CHRISTIAN WICCA

The Trinitarian Tradition

By

Nancy Chandler Pittman

ISBN: 1-4107-5348-4 (e-book)
ISBN: 1-4107-5347-6 (Paperback)

This book is printed on acid free paper.

1st Books - rev. 6/23/03

Acknowledgements

Blessed Be Our Christian Lord and Lady for letting us see the Light!

This book is dedicated to the devoted friends assembled on the
Christian Wicca yahoo group.
A world of thanks to my friend and Wiccan sister Kristina Mears, my
co-moderator, and my voice of reason and healthy conflict.

Loving thanks to my husband Dave, who allowed me the Luxury of
writing this book.
Special thanks to my Mom and Dad for raising me with plenty Of spirit
and pride for all that is right and the desire to go for any Goal that I set
for myself.
Thanks to them, my life has never had a dull moment.

~"Merry We Meet and Merry We Part:
As The Trinity Dwells within Our Heart"~
~"As above, so below. As within, so without.
As the Universe, so the Soul."~

Bide the Wiccan Law ye must,
In perfect love and perfect trust.
Eight words the Wiccan Rede fulfill:
An' ye harm none, do what ye will.

What ye send forth comes back to thee
So ever mind the law of three.
Follow this with mind and heart,
Merry ye meet, and merry ye part."

Blessed Be

Introduction

Christian Wicca is a new path of Christian spirituality and a new tradition of Wicca, often referred to as the modern term for the Old Religion, or "the religion of the wise." Christian Wicca is the practice of Wicca acknowledging the Christian Godhead as the practitioner's choice of Deities, recognizing both the male (God) and female (Goddess) aspects of the One Triune God, as well as the promised Solar God (Jesus), Lord and Saviour.

Wicca is the revival of the religion of the wise, recapturing its spirit and practices. This modern practice is based on the old ways of communing with the Divine through Nature, along the lines of the Latin phrase *Deus et Natura*, meaning "God and Nature." Originally, this religion did not have a name; it was simply what the people were brought up to believe. It was not called witchcraft with all its negative associations until the Inquisition found it to be a threat to the rise of the new Religion in Rome called Christianity.

The term *Wicca* is derived from the old Anglo-Saxon word *"wicce,"* (pronounced "witch-eee") and there you can see what gave rise to the commonly used word "witch." *"Wicce"* meant a practitioner of the Old Religion, as well as reflects the influence of the Old Norse word "vitke," which meant *"a priestess or seer."* The word pagan is from the Latin *"paganus,"* which means *"a country dweller."* *"Heathen,"* another related term also misinterpreted, which means *"one who dwelt on the heath."* The heath would be the plains or flatlands.

The writings and teachings of Gerald Gardner of the New Forest coven in England mark the dawning of Wicca. After the last of the anti-witchcraft laws in England were repealed in 1954, Gardner published his coven's Book of Shadows along with others believing that the Craft was dying out. He dedicated his life to retrieving lost information about the native religions of Europe. This was a difficult task because most of the old religion was handed down from generation to generation by mouth; keep in mind that most farming cultures could not read or write. Unlike Christianity, there was no "Bible" simply because the modern printing press had not been invented at the time!

This approach of communing with the Divine as the Holy Trinity via the personal spiritual methods of Wicca is the key to the name of this Wiccan tradition - *Trinitarian*. The definition of Trinitarian Wicca is as an eclectic form of Wicca mixed with various aspects of Christianity, which may differ with each practitioner. These sources of Christianity include the Holy Bible, the Kabbalah, the Apocrypha, Pseudopigrapha, and the Dead Sea Scrolls, especially the Gnostic Gospels.

Not all of the Judeo-Christian books written actually made it into the Holy Bible. For example, the Apocrypha is a generalized term for any spiritual writings that are doubtful of authenticity or of questionable authorship. The Books of the Apocrypha are the fourteen books of the Septuagint, or the Greek version of the Old Testament. Judaism rejects the Apocrypha, as does Protestant Christians, who regard is as non-canonical. However, the Roman Catholic Church fully accepts eleven of the writings into the canonized Catholic Bible.

The Pseudopigrapha is a group of early writings not included in either the canonized Bible or the Apocrypha. The *"pseudo"* aspect of the word denotes that these writings were fictitious or written with the intent to deceive by ascribing them as writings of popular characters of the Bible. The major difference of the Apocrypha and the Pseudopigrapha is that the authorship of the Apocrypha is uncertain. On the other hand, the authorship of the Pseudopigrapha is presumed to be written under the false names of famous prophets and key figures from the Old Testament.

The word "canon" comes from the Greek word *kanon*, a rod used to measure. The meaning of canon applied to the Bible is a list of books considered the true authoritative scripture by a particular religious sect.

This is a very important time in the history of Christianity. The Dead Sea Scrolls uncovered answers to many questions that the world has asked for over two thousand years. The cover up of so many mistruths about Christ and the early Church is causing the world to rethink organized religion. Many people are turning to Wicca, but they are *not* turning away from Christ. This is going to be the most difficult point for fundamental Christians to accept. The need for the presence of Jesus with the cosmic balance of a Heavenly Mother as well as a Heavenly Father is the new pathway to the Christian Divine - and many are taking this pathway by the means of Wicca.

The term *eclectic* is often associated with Wicca. It is best defined as selecting and composing spiritual knowledge from various spiritual sources, magio-religious systems, and doctrines of enlightenment that brings the practitioner closer to the One True Creative Spirit.

The eclecticism of spirituality is becoming more and more prevalent in our society today as spiritual seekers of knowledge are becoming increasingly aware that there is no "single true way" of enlightenment nor is there any one single religion that has all the answers to the meaning of this life and the after life. It deals with the simple fact that there is no one single book of prophecy and enlightenment, which does not contain contradictions or missing aspects of seemingly pertinent information. The most realistic reason for these contradictions is not "blamed on God," but the fact that man has tampered with Holy Scriptures for various reasons and humankind is imperfect. To gain perfection and be more like the Divine is the reason for religion. It is said that religion is the act of "re-legion" with the One True God; psychologist and spiritualist Carl Jung believes this to be one of humankind's basic natural instincts.

Another term often associated with Christian Wicca is *esoteric*. Specific spiritual ideas, literature, and doctrines intended for and only understood by a select group of individuals is the practical definition of this term. Its definition also includes information understood by an inner group of disciples or initiates, in reference to an organization it refers to those who study spiritual knowledge and practices beyond the understanding of the average religious practitioner. Esoterica deals with abstract spiritual thought, study, and meditations for positive results, greater understanding, and ultimate communion with the Divine.

Necessity is the mother of invention. While this is a common phrase and philosophy, perhaps this is the first time that the invention is not material. Trinitarian Wicca is an invention that deals with spirituality, not the inventions of physical ideas made manifest on the material plane. The spiritual necessity in this case is that young people are not getting what they need in their spiritual diet from organized Christian churches. Christian Wicca is the invention, which has self-manifested as a direct result of this emptiness concerning the soul which continues to look to the Judeo-Christian Pantheon, most specifically Jesus Christ and the recovery of the Feminine aspect of God.

Anyone with open eyes and an open mind can see that teenagers now fill New Age isles in the literary chain stores. Metaphysical bookstores are springing up everywhere as the youth of today are seeking a form of spirituality that their own fundamental Christian churches are not providing.

These are normal youths. I am not speaking of rebellious teenagers, drug addicts, and social misfits. I am speaking of the "kids next door." They are not seeking affiliation with dark entities, exerting power over others or involvement with Satanism; instead, they are simply looking for spiritual peace and balance in their lives. Why are today's youth looking for spiritual peace and balance in non-Christian based religions? It is simple; the Modern Church in any form or denomination is not doing its job! It is not providing spiritual peace and balance.

This should be a warning sign to all of Christianity! Alarms should be going off to the Modern Church, telling the Church leaders that something is dreadfully wrong in their organizations' spirituality departments. The Modern Organized Christian Churches are letting their young people down; as a direct result, people are looking for spiritual wholeness in the earth-based religions.

The younger generations have not been so pleased with what organized Christian religion has offered; they have many unanswered questions. What these generations now see in organized religion is not inner peace, love, and understanding. The church is now viewed as a facade for hypocrites, embezzlers, and users and squeezers; they have made the House of God a medium for comfortable business transactions within their own community, while moral charades are carried on in the name of saving people's souls on prime time television.

So, what happened to cause this change in the system of Organized Religion? Why are the newer generations finding no comfort in "the church"? Fundamental Christianity seemed to be so right for our parents and grandparents. What happened? Perhaps it is because those born starting in the 1940s (often referred to as the "baby boomers") were one of the first generations to have easy, widespread access to higher education, more solid world communication, and ready access to more news and information on more subjects. Therefore, since the middle of the 20th century, people have been entering the world with more choices, and they have had a better view of what they wanted simply because they were aware of more options. No longer did the family unit stay simple and isolated "down on the farm"; the scales of supply and demand were tilting and the material world took its toll on spirituality.

In the interviews for this book, I questioned family, friends, and acquaintances, both young and old. I questioned why Organized Religion has in fact hardened their hearts. The first response came from an immediate family member with "I am just not interested in getting into that," and they hung up. The next call produced an even more stinging answer: "What do those people have that I don't? At least I get to sleep late while they are chasing an old fairy tale every Sunday." To say the least, I was very surprised.

A more solid and intellectual take was given as "I think people today are not so different from our grandparents, but it takes life dealing you a bad hand from time to time and a great deal of mental baggage to make older persons finally turn to the church. This is a recurring cycle and the Baby Boomers and Generation X (those born during the 60's) just aren't to that point yet."

Then came one very simple answer that I tend to agree with: "... along with more opportunities for educational and world wide communication... we have more things that sizzle and pop and shine in our lives to hold our attention than the church."

What is the appeal of the earth-based religions?

The spiritual aspect of the Earth-based resurgence is affected primarily by the empty dogma and conjecture that fills the Protestants faiths and the Roman Catholic Church. The heart of the Organized Church is cold and without feeling. Institutionalized religion is not the basis of Earth re-affirming spiritualists. Wicca does not require debate within the denominations. Politics of who is the minister, who are the deacons and the elders, are not focal points of interest. Earth-based forms of spirituality are not monetarily based organizations, and there are no meetings about raising money for Youth Centers, new parking lots, nurseries, new carpet, or the remodeling of the building in which the services are held. Why commune with the Divine in a building, when the Earth is the embodiment of the Creator?

Wicca and other earth-based religions look to the Earth itself, and to nature as the visible form of the Creator of all things. Both young and old are looking to Wicca as the answer. Practitioners of the Old Religion grow in numbers each year. The ecological problems addressing the world today are forcing people to become aware of the value of the Earth and all living things. Deforestation, global warming, and the constant reduction of natural resources is causing our society to take a more serious look at the Earth and all the life-preserving importance of Nature. Thus, the importance of the reaffirmation of our planet now shows itself, perhaps, for the first time in thousands of years. The level of this importance is resulting in the Deification of the Earth, which is a return to the Goddess-oriented religions of the Ancients. The ecological crisis at hand is causing this generation to realize the interconnection of humankind and nature. Thus, we are witnessing the combination of spirituality, ecology, and politics in many new ways. This strongly affects the youth of today because *theirs* is the uncertain future.

Sociologically, people of all lifestyles and occupations are feeling the intensity of the times. Everywhere you turn, there are common complaints of the lack of hours in the day to work, sleep, and eat - there is even less hours to spend adequate time with family, exercise, or have a hobby. Therefore, with the ever-increasing technological acceleration of this world, our lives are increasing in complexity. We all have cell phones, computers, and home theatre systems. This generation has more advanced luxuries and scientific amenities than any other generation, yet we are more spiritually unfulfilled than any generation in history.

So, how does spirituality and religion fit into the modern equation? Simple, it doesn't. Religion is being replaced by spirituality. As lengthy church services are becoming more difficult to fit into our modern schedules, we are searching for a new way to commune with the Divine. Many are counterbalancing the need for religion with nature-based spirituality.

It seems the more complex our physical lives become the simpler our metaphysical or spiritual lives become. Hermetic Law dictates that for every action, there is an equal and opposite reaction. With the onset of modern technology and every aspect of our life is "on full-tilt - 24/7", we need some aspect of our lives to be calm, gentle, and simple

This does not mean that we are too busy for "God," but instead that we are a product of the demands of our modern, fast paced age. Many people work two jobs now to afford the basic necessities of life. Married couples hardly have time for their families - let alone, time to get dressed up and attend Church. The time spent in church is valuable time that can be used more efficiently in personal meditation and private communion with the Divine. This form of spirituality can be achieved without the intercession of institutionalized religion.

Ironically, more times than not, young Christians are finding a closer relationship to the Christian Divine through the worship and meditative techniques of Wicca than they did through their former churches, regardless of denomination or religious preference. Wicca was once a Pagan-only spiritual path. However, during this time of spiritual revolution, it is quite common to hear practitioners profess that "Jesus led me to Wicca."

After many years of research and participation in the Wiccan community, I discovered that today's young people are lacking the same spiritual completion as myself; the only difference being that I am twenty years older. I also felt the emptiness that the Modern Church has offered their congregations. It seemed something was missing, but I did not know what. It seemed that most religions are based in fear, creating a "worship me or burn" mentality. This did not coincide with the spiritual laws of free will and the positive messages taught by Jesus during his time on earth.

Being an American citizen, I knew that religious freedom was one of the founding principles of our great nation. This principle includes freedom of religion, as well as freedom from religion - It also includes freedom from religious persecution - which isn't happening! Fundamental Christians support religious freedom as long as it supports their particular branch of Christianity.

Over hundreds of years, the scare tactics of Christianity never reflected an ethical and loving interpretation of The Bible. Instead, the inter-faith hatred seemed totally opposite of the messages of love, spoken by the Living Jesus.

Hatred, prejudice, and bigotry are ugly displays of emotion in any setting. When these nasty traits weave their way into religion; it is a miracle anyone has faith in anything.

One of the greatest spiritual compliments I have ever received came from my husband: "You love Jesus not *because* of the Organized Church *but in spite* of the Organized Church!" The more I thought about that statement the more I pondered. I could not help but wonder if I was the only one who had such thoughts. Did others feel this way? At first, I shyly began to delve into books of research, not really making my quest known to anyone.

The first thing I realized was that no tradition of Wicca extended any set of complications in order to commune with the Divine One Spirit. That simplicity is the key to the rise in popularity of the modern form of the Old Religion. The dogma of Wicca totally boiled down to eight words "An' it harm none, do what ye wilt." Wicca encourages people to live a good life and be good to their fellow human beings not because an all powerful God was threatening them with going to Hell, but because living a good life is the right thing to do for oneself and for all involved in a person's life.

Already, you have probably noticed the term "tradition" which is often affiliated with Wicca. Do not let this word make you uncomfortable as a follower of the teachings of Christ. The word tradition simply means "teaching" and it is not exclusive to Wicca or the Old Religion of pre-Christian Europe; the term tradition also is primarily associated with the definition and concept of oral teachings. The Apostolic Tradition exists in Christianity and it is defined as the teachings which originated with Jesus and his twelve apostles. This term indicated that one could preach the truth orally; likewise, anyone could learn by simply listening to the oral teachings of the apostles. It is the oral presentation of scriptural truth, or the codifying of biblical truth into creedal expression.

While it is true that the early Church held to the concept of Tradition as referring to ecclesiastical customs and practices, don't forget that at one time the Bible was not assembled. We take a leap of faith that the words of the Bible are the correct interpretations of the Apostolic Tradition. Nevertheless, many of these doctrines of the faith conflicted with each other within the Bible and each religious sect has their own view and interpretation of the Bible.

An example of this interfaith contradiction can be found early on, in the second century in the controversy over the correct day to celebrate Easter. Certain Eastern churches celebrated it on a particular day, while the Western Churches celebrated it on a different day. Both churches respectively believed that their particular practice was handed down to them directly from the Apostles. Each of the early Christian sects believed their doctrine to be the only one. In reality, they argued over the letter of the law, while obviously both were the "spirit of the law."

Doesn't Wicca Require Pagan Deities?

I was attracted to Wicca; however, I was not comfortable calling upon Deities other than the Christian Trinity. Due to the manner in which Greek and Roman mythology was taught in my local school systems, gods and goddesses which are considered pagan seemed more like fiction and less like a realistic choice for the male and female principle of The Divine. I did not yet understand the concept of godforms, human archetypes, and anthropomorphism. Needless to say, I was very confused.

I realize spirituality is not an issue that anyone should take lightly. Therefore, I tried to analyze my motives and search within myself for selfish reasoning. Yet, I kept coming back to the problem of asking myself "how could I feel better *and* worse at the same time about my choice of spiritual paths?"

If I attend a Modern Christian church every Sunday, I would be lying not only to myself but also to the Divine Creator of the Universe. I could not imagine that living a lie was the point of "going to church." Yet, if I started to worship Gods and Goddesses that seemed mythological, I would still be lying to myself because Jesus would not be involved in my ceremonies and rituals, and eliminating Jesus was not the point of this spiritual exercise.

I have always been attracted to Catholicism from afar, but never acted on attending because I felt like I would be a "beginner" and I felt alone in my struggle. I loved their elaborate ceremonies, the candles, and the incense, but I really didn't know why. Since my youth, I faithfully watched the televised event of Midnight Mass at the Vatican on Christmas Eve. I watched it mostly for the beginning ceremony; it was fascinating to me that these people put so much forethought and preparation into their religious gatherings. It wasn't that way at any of the churches I had attended, regardless of the minister. All I had to do to go to church was put on an appropriate dress and sit and listen to the preacher. Sure there was singing, praying, and communion but somehow, that did not have the same impact. I didn't know why I loved this ceremony so much until I started this research. as I grew up in a loving Christian home, but Protestant none the less.

In retrospect, I realize now the underlying rituals of the Old Religion was the attraction of Catholicism. They praised Jesus and the Father while quietly acknowledging Mary as the Mother of God - not quite a Goddess, but the next best thing to filling the need for a Heavenly Mother. I knew that many of the Saints were angels (which I adore!) and cultural deities of the Old Religion were granted sainthood in exchange for Pagan cultures converting to Christianity. Yet, deep down inside, I knew what I was looking for was not in a church building.

I loved the elaborate Christianized rituals that Catholicism presented. I found the unsurpassed dedication to Mary, the pseudo-Goddess of Catholicism, to be comforting along side the Father, Son, and the Holy Spirit. Regardless, all the dogmatic trappings of Fundamental Christianity were still present! I began to feel, that if a church building was in the equation at all, (the physical structure itself), I felt some sort of spiritual claustrophobia. It seemed that the church building had become the embodiment of man-made religion and everything that spirituality was NOT suppose to be! that simply did not seem to be "the Will of God" but the will of whoever was passing the collection plate.

I did not know what to do. I loved Jesus - no problems there. Because I am female, I knew that part of "God" had to be a Goddess! After all, Genesis 1:26-27 says: "And God said, Let us make man in our own image, after our likeness ... So God created man in his own image, in the image of God created he him; male and female created he them." Yet, knowing that God is the combined image of male and female, therefore being both male and female, the early church set about only acknowledging the male aspect of God, as thus became a "He".

Frustrated, I stepped away from the situation and looked at it objectively and realistically. I began to realize that the Modern Churches of Christianity today, both Protestant and Catholic do not make up the Christian Godhead - as the Gnostic Gospel of Thomas comments, "The Kingdom of God is inside you and all around you ... not in a building of wood and stone." Being a member of any organized Church does not make one a Christian, it is an individual's personal relationship with Jesus and the Holy Trinity that constitutes a Christian. A follower of the teachings of Christ is a Christian, not a person who attends a specific Organized Church.

I had found my answer finally! It had been staring me in the face the entire time and I was too blind to see it. One *can* worship Jesus, the Father, and the Holy Spirit (or the feminine aspect of the Divine) through Wicca in an equally viable manner as any other form of Christianity.

However, most Fundamental and dogmatic Christians will say this is wrong. Why is it wrong? Why can we not commune with Jesus, the Holy Mother and Father by observing the changing of the seasons and the cycles of the moon? Did the Divine not create these things? Why should I limit my spirituality?

Wicca is a spiritual path of attunement to nature. We seek to find the harmony and balance with nature, so we can have harmony and balance within; thus, we are more productive in life, our jobs and more loving and understanding of ourselves, our families and humanity as a whole. To achieve this, Wiccans celebrate eight festivals of the year called sabbats, which mark the changes of the seasons and the biorhythms of nature.

Likewise, Wiccans celebrate the cycles of the moon. There are 13 moons in a calendar year on a 28-day lunar cycle. Many people of all faiths experience insomnia, rage, or ignitability around the time of the full moon - thus the term "lunacy" from the Latin word "*luna*," meaning moon. Attuning your monthly body clock is helpful to combat all these things for any person. Due to the 28-day cycle, woman can find natural feminine health by participating in Lunar Rites. Soon, women will find their personal cycles flowing with the moons and not against it, and achieving physical and metaphysical balance within.

Wiccans do not worship the Earth, but instead honor it as the embodiment of Creation, the life-giving act that we should all respect and be thankful. The Sun and the Moon are equated with the Father and the Mother. In the day, look up and remember our God; at night, look up and remember our Goddess - they are with us all the time! The sun and the moon are not worshipped, but instead serve as nature's reminder that the Divine watches over us continuously.

Now, having stated these basic principles, realize that there is no specific Deity(s) required to practice Wicca. Instead, the different traditions allow for different Deity focuses. The Egyptians revered the Divine in the form of the Goddess Isis and the God Osiris, who gave birth to Horus. The Greeks favored Zeus and Hera, Cronos and Rhea, and Persephone and Hades. The Canaanites looked to Inanna and Tammuz; The Norse practitioners follow Freya and Odin, while Kernunnos and Diana were God and Goddess for many European traditions. Even the Native Americans observed the Moon Mother and Father Sky, similar to the other nature deities such as the Green Man and Mother Earth.

It is very important to Christian Wiccans to be accepted as serious practitioners. It is very important to Christian Wiccans that their choice of Lord and Lady is considered equally as viable as the ones mentioned above.

Church does not make a Christian

Practitioners of Organized and Fundamental Christianity are simply following the Catholic form of worship dictated by the Vatican, which is the mass. The Protestant form of worship basically consists of one person reading from the Bible or preaching the sermon as the rest of the followers of their faith sit and listen. The truth is that the average Christian churchgoers have no idea why they worship in the method that they do!

If you do not believe me, ask various people around you and see what type of answers you get. Ask these questions seriously: "Why do you pray here? Why sing at this part? Why can we not have Communion every time the doors are open?" While most of the answers to these questions seem to be flexible according to the various denominations, Jesus said (referring to Communion) "this do as often as you think of me" … so how many times a year do you think of Jesus? Do you think once a month is okay? Is it exactly at the time every Sunday after the Closing Thoughts/Benediction and before the sermon? Do you only think of Jesus on specific holidays? Is nodding off to sleep during the sermon really worshipping?

One aspect of the Organized Church that always bothered me is people who complain about the minister yet continue to attend the same church their entire lives. It seems to me, that if one does not like what the minister is saying, why does one continue to listen to this person? If you can present the message in a way that others might better comprehend, then why do you not do it? Why are you not the minister?

My next step was seeking others of like mind and spirit. I created an email list and a site on the Internet (http://www.christianwicca.com) featuring information for others attracted to Wicca, but who wish to still hold onto their Judeo-Christian beliefs. I was overwhelmed with the positive response from other spiritual seekers who believed as I did.

Christian Wiccans come from every denomination. While the doctrines of each believers' prior affiliation and upbringing are indeed deeply ingrained, the reason they have distanced themselves from their respective denomination is usually due to the lack of love and spiritual warmth they feel in these organized forms of Christianity. Instead, they have found this spiritual wholeness in Wicca. Organized dogma has overpowered the love and closeness to The Divine. This is the reason why Christian Wicca is on the rise; spiritual Christians no longer wish affiliation with the ways of Fundamentalism, which often leaves the individual empty handed and with an empty heart. Fundamental Churches have been too busy following the letter of the law to follow the spirit of the law. The religious teachings, principles, and faith in Jesus Christ are *not* the concepts from which

Christian Wiccans are fleeing; instead, it is the cold heart of the Organized Church and the absence of the love of a Heavenly Mother.

The teachings of Christ are as sacred to the Trinitarian path of Christianity as they are with any fundamentalist faith, however, Christian Wiccan's do not believe that any single version of the Bible, be it the 66 book Protestant Bible or the 72 book Catholic Bible, should be considered the only book of enlightenment. Trinitarian Wiccans should not wish to do away with The Bible as it stands today - but instead dig deeper and learn more! Christian Wiccans also take on the knowledge that is beneficial and applicable to each personally from additional texts such as the Apocrypha, the Pseudopigrapha, the Kabbalah, the Nag Hammadi Library/Dead Sea Scrolls, and the Torah and the Talmud. Christian Wiccans realize and acknowledge the Judaic origins in Christianity. Christian Wiccans also follow the 8-line version of the Wiccan Rede as shown below:

"Bide the Wiccan Law ye must,
In perfect love and perfect trust.
Eight words the Wiccan Rede fulfill:
An' ye harm none, do what ye will.

What ye send forth comes back to thee
So ever mind the law of three.
Follow this with mind and heart,
Merry ye meet, and merry ye part."

Don't let the Olde English way of speaking confuse you to the meaning of the Wiccan Rede; it is not far from the King James Version of English used in the Bible. The meaning is akin to Christian philosophies, such as "Do unto others as you would have them do unto you" and "love thy neighbor as you would thyself." Also, the old saying of "what goes around comes around" follows the laws of universal karma - what you do always comes back to you, whether it be good or bad.

So, Christian Wiccans have agreed to adapt to the basic principles of early Christianity: 1) honoring the Holy Trinity, 2) baptism, 3) communion, 4) strive to seek truth and love, and 5) to continue to read and study all forms of scriptures that each individual finds enlightening and as a guide to their Higher Selves.

Christian Wiccan or Witch?

A commonly asked question is "What is the difference between a Wiccan and a Witch?" The answer to this question differs from practitioner to practitioner. The reasons for the use of one of the terms over the other vary. As with any good situation, there can always be abuse of the same set of variables. Often young people enjoy the shock value of the word Witch, as well as do many older people who like to draw attention to them. Many are attracted to the romantic aura of exploring the mysteries of the occult and the paranormal. Such practitioners feel that Witch is the more accurate and descriptive term for their quest for universal understanding.

Many practitioners are proud of the term Witch, which to them is a title of spiritual knowledge, esoteric wisdom, and use it regardless of the negative connotations that started with the Burning Times of the Inquisition. Obviously, these practitioners of the Old Religion are strong and solid in their faith and the convictions of their spiritual path. Some practitioners believe that the term Wiccan is a G-rated compromise of the term for a practitioner of Witchcraft and that makes it merely a more palatable approach for the Western World, considering all the negative preconceptions about The Craft and the Old Religion.

Renowned Wiccan literary great Scott Cunningham stated in the linguistic notes of many of his books that *"though some use 'Wiccan' and 'Witch' almost interchangeably, I prefer the older less-encumbered word Wicca, and so use it almost exclusively."*

For the purposes of this book, the term Wicca is synonymous with religious practices and the path toward a more personalized and intimate spiritual relationship with the Divine, as well as a more fulfilling means of communing with the Great Creator Spirit. Likewise, for the purposes of this book - I find the term Witch more appropriately used as a practitioner of Witchcraft, or the craft of the witch. As always, these definitions vary from person to person, and author to author.

Spiritual Awakening

As we stand at the beginning of the twenty first century, many of us are experiencing spiritual enlightenment for the first times in our lives. Our higher selves are blossoming and we are feeling transformations of our heart and soul, giving us a new outlook on a life that is not so bleak.

Life is full of many natural metamorphoses; for the flora and the fauna of nature, they are born, grow and die, only to return the next year to start the cycle of life all over again. For nature, this process is gentle, peaceful, and beautiful. This natural metamorphosis goes without political and religious repercussions. Independent freethinking Christians who hunger for knowledge are like the spiritual butterfly emerging from the cocoon of organized religions, denominations, and sects.

The unusual thing about this spiritual awakening is there are so many people suddenly feeling the presence of a Female Deity, or the female principle of a monotheist Deity. This is not a Pagan feminine Deity or Goddess, but a Christian Goddess. A Goddess of the religion based on the life, example, and teachings of Jesus Christ. Millions are experiencing these feelings; it is comforting, and fulfilling. This spiritual movement seems to complete the voids and emptiness that organized religions have failed to provide us with for the last 50 years. It is safe to say that great hunger to recover the feminine aspect of the Divine is part of the answer to this spiritual awakening.

Today, Modern Christians are recognizing the gap they feel in their heart and soul is the lack of love provided by the balance within of a Male and a Female aspect of God. Many spiritually aware Christians look to the Holy Spirit as the Mother God. I uncovered many parallels surrounding the faceless Holy Spirit of the New Testament during my quest for information on The GodPair (or the Mother-Father Deity that is at one time both male and female). I have noticed that more often than not, theologians and divinity graduates believe that the Spirit, acknowledged as the Spirit of God, the Wisdom of God in the Old Testament and as the Holy Spirit in the New Testament, is the female principle of the Christian Trinity.

The Holy Spirit is usually the Goddess recognized by Christian Wiccans from Protestant backgrounds. Due to the influences of the Kabbalah and Gnosticism, Christian Wiccans believe in the existence of the Mother-Father Principles of The High God, or the Male and Females halves of The All or "the Divine Us." So you may hear some speak of the Shekinah, Asherah/Innana, Eloah or Eloi: the feminine half of Elohim, Sophia, The Holy Spirit, the Virgin Mary, or Mary Magdalene, in regards to being the female aspect of the genderless God or The Divine. All of these names represent different aspects of the Christian Goddess. However, the Goddess of Christianity that you acknowledge usually depends on one's religious upbringing, amount of non-dogmatic religious study, personal spiritual beliefs and the culmination of all of these aspects.

There is a spiritual feeling of love in the heart and the comfortable arms of the Divine. This spiritual awakening is embracing everyone like a child, telling you that everything is going to be just fine. In addition, for the first time in so many people's life they can proudly say "I am a Christian and I feel the Spirit, the Word, the Trinity - I feel the Divine: This is spiritually right".

This spiritual revolution is not something that I alone "dreamed up." Students of esoteric knowledge should be familiar with the concept of the changing of great spiritual periods throughout history, however - we are simply the generation to be aware, involved in, and affected by this magicko-religious changing of the guard. Thanks to the 1971 musical, "Hair," we are all familiar with the lyrics that state: "This is the dawning of the Age of Aquarius." However, it is not just a psychedelic song or musical New Age rhetoric.

The length of the cycle of the astrological calendar is approximately 26,000 years. It is divided into twelve periods of approximately 2,150 years and 30 days. Each period coincides with the twelve signs of the zodiac. The ages travel backwards, not forward, as most would think. This is because our Sun does not quite make it back to the starting point each year, and it gives the appearance of slowly moving backward through the zodiac.

The correspondences of the Piscean Age stand true; there are many symbols of "fish and water" surrounding Jesus and His teachings. Symbolisms such as the Ichthus Fish displaying the initial letters of the Greek phrase "Jesus Christ, Son of God, Savior" form the Greek word ICHTHUS, which means "fish."

Jesus encouraged His disciples to be "fishers of men." The fish and correspondences continue with the feeding the multitude with five loaves and two fishes, walking on water, and the importance of symbolic rebirth by baptism of water and spirit.

Other Christian correspondences of the spiritual ages were the observations of the 12th century monk Joachim de Fiote, who postulates the existence of three great ages that correspond to the Father, the Son, and the Holy Spirit. The era of The Father is the Old Testament times marked by the creation, giving of the law, and the words of the prophets. The era of the Son is the New Testament times marked by the birth, death, and resurrection of Jesus Christ, His life of teachings, the Gospels and the assembly of the earliest stages of the Christian church. The era of the Holy Spirit marks the duality of the diminishing existence of the organized church with the acceleration of personal spirituality - when individual would be driven by the love of the Spirit and commune directly with the Divine. Joachim de Fiote believed this to be the spiritual age foretold in Christ's teachings and parables.

It does not matter if you believe in the existence and practice of these hybrid paths of spirituality or agree with their existence because there is an increasing subgroup within both Paganism and Christianity. Until Christian Wicca appeared on the spiritual scene, a common saying was "not all Pagans are Wiccans, but all Wiccans are Pagan." Well, now that has changed! Now, not all Wiccans are Pagans ... many Wiccans are Christians! The names of the Creator/Creatrix may differ and the methods of worship may vary, but the pure intent of spiritual unity with The Divine remains the same and is the prime focus.

These are very exciting spiritual times for the Spiritual Community as hybrid paths are pulling together, creating a middle ground of mutual beliefs and parallels between the two extremes, and ironically, finding that there is not much difference at all.

Actually, blending of Catholicism and various forms of the Old Religion has been around for centuries. Santeria is probably the most common hybrid religion, hiding the Yoruba and Afro-Caribbean Gods within the Catholic saints gave rise to this path that literally means "the way of the saints." Likewise, many European practitioners of the craft, such as the Strega, often acknowledge the duality of their Native faith with their attendance at the Catholic Church by having two altars in their home: one dedicated to the religion of their ancestors and one to the new Christian religion of Rome.

I feel that at this point, it should be pointed out that the term Pagan did not originally mean "anti-Christian," this aspect of the definition of Pagan is a product of falsehoods contrived by the Early Church Fathers. The term *pagan* pre-dates Christianity; it comes from the Latin term "paganus" meaning "country dweller." It is but one of the bastardized terms that came about in order to spread fear, confusion, and more efficiently establish the Orthodox Christian Church throughout the world. Oddly enough, many Neo-Pagans have started accepting the "anti-Christian" definition, not according to their Pagan roots but as defined by the Roman Catholic Church and mainstream Christianity.

Those in this spiritual subculture bear names such as Christian Wiccans, Trinitarian Wiccans, ChristoWiccans, ChristoPagans, Goddess Christians, Eco-Christians, Green Christians, Eclectic Christians, Kabballistic Wiccans, Gnostic Christians, Gnostic Wiccans, Grail Priests, WicCatholics, EpiscoPagans, Pagans for Jesus, JeWitches, Christian Craft Practitioners and Christian Witches. My on-going research produces more and more subculture names each day. Likewise, there are practitioners of the Old

Religion coupled with a form of Christianity, who have one foot in both worlds but do not yet know what to call themselves.

In the book, "The Crafted Cup," the author Shadwynn speaks of his affiliated organization called Ordo Arcanorum Gradalis. This group incorporates many belief systems, mentioning "Pagan Celtic, Roman, Greek, and Mediterranean influences along with the rich streams of Gnosticism and esoteric Christianity." However, he goes on to say that "for many within the Wiccan spectrum of belief this kind of religious syncretism is threatening, for it forces them to acknowledge the validity of the Judeo-Christian mystical traditions, something which many Wiccans and Neo-Pagans are most reluctant to do, due to their latent Christophobia."

These communities are composed of members who are extremely familiar with the Holy Bible and relevant scholarship, other books of enlightenment such as the Torah and the Talmud, the Holy Kabbalah and the Dead Sea Scrolls. These seekers of spiritual completion are usually familiar with key figures in religious history and the politics of the era. Then, with all this religious and historical research, they are also living a more personal spiritual path of an earth-based religion.

This type of spiritual upheaval does not go on without fears, paranoia, and the worry of "am I doing the right thing?" Any new school of thought meets with as much opposition as support, which is only natural. Many times the opposition is not about the new school of thought, but one's own opposition to making any changes in their own lives.

The change in spirituality seemingly is affecting the Christians the strongest, and these feelings are ones that apparently all are experiencing in the same way. Just as a quick note, many followers of Islam are also putting the female aspect of Allat back along side of Allah, who disappeared with the emergence of Mohammad - in many ways identical to the Hebrew Goddess losing prominence with the advent of Christianity.

Some spiritualists and theologians point out that perhaps Christianity has come full circle, and the female spirit is being put back into the Trinity, after being edited out of the Bible for over a thousand years. Once again, people are speaking of "The Old Religion" and the simplicities of worshipping The Divine and living in harmony with nature and the Heavenly Hosts. Increasingly, practitioners are becoming celestially minded and spending time in study and meditation, both in private and with others in their area who are following the Wiccan path with the Judeo-Christian understanding of The Trinity.

One cannot place gender limitations on this Supreme Being. Instead, it transcends and yet encompasses both human genders. If The All were simply male, then it would be limited; if The All were simply female, then it would be limited. It is limiting both in our ability to comprehend The All, to express The All-self to our own being and it is limiting in our ability to identify with The All, simply in the most general aspects. The whole point behind the Judeo-Christian Divine is that it is not limited, but that it is the great I AM, a Being that encompasses and transcends *all*! This transcendence includes us. This is why so many Christian spiritualists feel that the combination of Wicca and Judeo-Christianity works so well together. Traditional Christianity has viewed God as a solely masculine figure for a very long time; to many the concept of God as a feminine figure seems blasphemous. While as Christians, we know that we should not judge others; we must recognize that the translators of the Bible were "only human" - we should not dwell on the male aspect of the translators and the gender bias. It is the 21st century and we should have all advanced past the mindset of the Middle Ages. Regardless of their gender, religious affiliates have placed limits on the limitless Divine and by doing this Christianity and its adherents have suffered.

From a September 10, 1999 article entitled "The Papal Positions on a Feminine Deity" in the Times of London: "The Pope, who this year said that God was not 'an old man with a white beard', went a step further yesterday and referred to 'God the Mother'. The Pope, regarded as dogmatically conservative and patriarchal, has surprised critics this year with uncharacteristically open-minded revisions of doctrine as part of his preparations for a Christian mission in the new millennium. He is keen to broaden the appeal of Christianity, his advisers say, and to ensure that no sections of society feel "left out of its all-embracing message." The Pope has clashed with feminists and remains opposed to the ordination of women. However, he praised the "vital role" of women in the Roman Catholic Church, and talks with reverence of his own mother, Emilia, who died when he was nine in Poland. The Pope is also a devotee of the cult of the Virgin Mary, although she is referred to as the Mother of God, and not as a God Mother, since she does not share the divinity of God and Christ. The Lord's Prayer opens with the words "Our Father, which art in heaven", and in the Gospel of St Matthew, Jesus says: "Everything is entrusted to me by my Father; and no one knows the Son but the Father, and no one knows the Father but the Son" (Matthew 11:27). Nevertheless, speaking to pilgrims in St Peter's Square, the Pope said God had both a male and female nature. Reflecting on the forgiveness of sins, he said: "The hands of God hold us up, they hold us tight, they give us strength. Nevertheless, at the same time they give us comfort, they console and caress us. They are the hands of a Father and a Mother at the same time." The Pope said the parable of the prodigal son reflected this dual nature, with the father in the story disciplining his son and even throwing him out, but later welcoming him back. The pontiff said the capacity to forgive those who repented was, if anything, more a female trait than a male one. Theologians said that in admitting that God had a "feminine side" the Pope was conscious of a remark made by his predecessor, Pope John Paul I, who in 1978 astonished pilgrims by remarking that God was "the Father, but is also the Mother". Liberal theologians such as Dr. Hans Kung, who was forbidden to teach theology 20 years ago after repeatedly defying Vatican edicts, welcomed the Pope's latest remarks. He said that it was time to acknowledge that God "transcends the sexes."

As we read in the previous quote, even Pope John Paul II has come forward and proclaimed "God the Mother" as correct an interpretation as "God the Father." To say the Divine is not equally feminine is heretical; the Judeo-Christian Deity finds no limit in gender, age, race or any other earthly confines that we tend to assign.

The Spirit of modern Wicca has been acknowledging this fact for centuries, since it takes into account a God and a Goddess, a literal cosmic balance and subsidiary of The All or The High God. Wicca acknowledges that both polarities are an expression of the Great Divine; therein lies its strength, as well as its adaptability with the teachings of Christianity.

The Female Aspect of God:
Supporting Scriptures

"Whatever is hidden
Is meant to be disclosed.
And whatever is concealed
Is meant to be brought into the open"
(Mark 4:22)

Most of the information of any Female Deity or feminine affiliation with the Godhead is absent from the Holy Bible, but only on the surface. That is one possibility as to why the Bible contradicts itself and if you read in your own Bible's Concordance, most have information about the contradictions and various opinions on the subject.

The first nine chapters of Proverbs are dedicated to Sophia, however the English translation notes Her only as the Spirit Wisdom, or Lady Wisdom. Wisdom is referred to as "She" throughout the book *Proverbs*, found in both the Catholic and Protestant Bible.

The Apocrypha, which contains 14 books of the sacred literature of the Alexandrian Jews, also includes *The Wisdom of Solomon*. This book also gives great account of Sophia. In addition, Chapter 24 of *Ecclesiasticus* or *Sirach* speaks warmly of Lady Wisdom or Sophia; verse 9 tells of Her creation: "He created me from the beginning before the world, and I shall never fail." Verse 18 states Her position as the helpmate of the Creator:

"I am the Mother of fair love, of fear, and knowledge,
and holy hope: I therefore, being eternal, am given to all my
children, which are named by Him."

Proverbs 3:13-19 reveals Lady Wisdom's :

"Happy is the man that findeth Wisdom, and the man
that getteth understanding: for the merchandise of it is better
Than the merchandise of silver, and the gain thereof than
Fine gold. She is more precious than rubies; and all the
Things thou canst desire are not to be compared to her.
Length of days is in her right hand; and in her left hand,
Riches and Honor. Her ways are pleasantness and
All her paths are peace.
She is a Tree of Life to them that lay

> *Hold upon her; and happy*
> *Is everyone that retaineth her.*
> *The lord by Wisdom has founded the earth;*
> *By understanding hath he established the heavens. "*

Aside from verses such as these, the Dead Sea Scrolls uncovered most of the information of The Feminine Divine in the upper portions of the Nile River; while other tidbits of information have been random lines of text in the Apocrypha and the Pseudopigrapha. Some of the most revealing books regarding the Christian Goddess, Great Mother, or female aspect of the Divine Creator are found among the various writings found at Nag Hammadi, Egypt.

We can attribute the discovery of the first manuscripts in 1945 to two Egyptian farmers. They discovered these long lost writings in a cave at Khirbat Qumran on the northwest shore of the Dead Sea in Jordan. They were searching for natural fertilizer when these farmers found the sealed jars. By the farmers' own admission, at first they were afraid to open the jars because of the local superstitions that a frightening or harmful entity might be dwelling within. Later were overcome with greed after realizing their proximity to the gold treasures located not far from them in the Valley of the Kings, and they proceeded to open the sealed jars.

Ironically, while it was not gold that these farmers found within the clay pots, a treasure surprised, shocked, and overwhelmed the Christian world of the twentieth century. These clay pots contained additional Gospels, Apocalypses, and additional Books of Acts written by the other disciples but not included due to their acknowledgement of the Goddesses, expressly Sophia and the Holy Spirit. Some of these texts are collectively part of the Gnostic Gospels, while others are ancient writings obviously spiritual in nature but have not necessarily fallen into any singular ethnic category.

Many of the codices fell to ruin due to natural decay and fragmentation. Others may have been stolen, lost, or inadvertently destroyed. There is confusion over the blending of times, writing styles and indigenous regional characteristics often found within the *same* collective writing. The languages of these books include ancient Hebrew, Aramaic, and Greek. By 1947, approximately 400 manuscripts had been discovered with writings that date from 100 BC to 68 AD.

Some of the manuscripts discovered exhibit the writing characteristics of the ancient Jewish sects, the Essenes, and the Ebionites. The books having the most impact on Modern day Christianity come from the Gnostic Christians, who flourished about 2,000 years ago. These were some of the first Christians put to death, perhaps not for their acknowledgement of Jesus, but for their belief in both a Mother & Father Deity as the Heavenly parents of Christ. The concept of the Mother God was too close to Paganism for the New Christian Church and the Emperor Constantine.

The loss of the Alexandrian Library is one of the greatest tragedies of history. It was the largest and most famous of all the ancient collections of written knowledge. The Egyptian Ruler, Ptolemy I, began this library in 200 B.C.E.; other rulers contributed to the Library until it contained over 500,000 books. Part of the Library was lost during the siege of Julius Caesar in 47 B.C.E. and the many sieges that followed; one of the hardest attacks came from the Muslims. Most of these texts were thought to be destroyed within the auxiliary Library of Alexandria in Egypt in AD 391 by the Orthodox Christians. The Orthodox Christians were determined to wipe out what they considered "pagan learning." Arabs completed the destruction in 640 ADE.

Constantine was calling for religious uniformity throughout the empire. This uniformity was for the good of Constantine and his Empire and definitely not necessarily for the common good of overall Christianity. This assault on the contents of the canonized Bible put stress on the translators and the councils responsible for the chosen books. Throughout this assault, Nero, Constantine and the other emperors continued to destroy any texts that did not work to the benefit of the newly forming Orthodox Church in Rome. Unfortunately in their haste to destroy documents that did not support the decisions of the Roman councils, many scrolls were destroyed that were not Biblical in nature, such as the works of Aristotle and Plato were destroyed. Marc Anthony alone took 200,000 scrolls from Pergamum in 41 B.C.E. and gave them to Cleopatra at Alexandria.

The goal of the Alexandrian library staff was to collect the best of the world's literature that passed through Egypt. All persons visiting Egypt at this time possessing literary and artistic works, inventions, and blueprints would have their works temporarily obtained by the workers of the Alexandrian Library, have their work copied with utmost care and accuracy, and then returned before leaving the country. In modern terms, the Library of Alexandria worked much like the United States patent office.

The original manuscripts of the Gnostic Gospels were written in the colloquial dialects of Aramaic, Hebrew, and Greek. Attacks on early Christian worship sites appear to be the places in which the manuscripts were obliterated. The urgent closure of the canonization of the scriptures was called for of demands made by the newly converted Roman Emperor Constantine. Dedicated Egyptian Christian Monks, or the Coptic Christians, worked secretly and urgently in poorly lit cells and caves to save these sacred writings. They never realized the fruits of their labor would lay dormant for two thousand years, only to be discovered and declared heresy.

The Nag Hammadi scrolls were either buried on purpose, or buried by massive sandstorms. Additional copies of these scrolls or codices have also been scattered throughout the world for safekeeping. They have been found in hidden rooms in places such as St. Catherine's Monastery on Mt. Sinai in the 500's A.C.E,. at St. Gall in Switzerland in the 600's A.C.E., and in the 800's A.C.E. at the Holy Mount in Atos, Greece.

An Overview of the Kabbalah, the Gnostic Gospels, and Wicca

"Be a lamp to yourself.
Be your own confidence.
Hold to the truth within yourself,
As to the only Truth" —— Buddha

In the introduction of this book, I begin to explain the concept of Christian Wicca. A Christian or a follower of Jesus can find the Female aspect of the Divine in the Kabbalah and the Gnostic Gospels. Once the role of a Christian Goddess can be determined then, She can be placed along side of the Orthodox Christian God and Son. Once this cosmic balance is established, the Christian Goddess and God can be applied to the ceremonies and ritual techniques of Traditional Wicca, which has never included a Christian Female Deity.

Since it is impossible to grasp Christian Wicca without first understanding each of its components, I have assembled an overview of each topic. The following gives generalized ideas, principles, and insight as to how the pieces of the puzzle all fit together.

Wiccans, Gnostics, and Kabbalahists alike worship a Divine Goddess and a God whom they understand as separate but equal manifestations of The All, Spirit, Akasha, the High God, or the "Unknown Deity."

Kabbalahists recognize The Supernal Father as Yahweh and The Supernal Mother as Elohim, the God and Goddess who stems from the genderless Supreme Being pronounced Eheieh. The Gnostic Christians regarded Sophia as the female principle of The All, while the male principle is nameless but addressed as the Good Father.

The origins of Wicca, as we celebrate today are indigenous to greater Western Europe. The followers of pre-Gardnerian Wicca were very earth-oriented as farmers and hunters, who recognized the anthropomorphic representation of The High God. Many Fundamental Christians can understand the concepts of Wicca as similar to the Shamanistic aspects of the Native American Indians, who honor Father Sky and Mother Earth (and Mother Moon who watched over them at night while Father Sun rested).

There are many names for the Goddess due to Her questionable position in the Trinity as scholars and translators have manipulated most of the Judeo-Christian Holy Writings. For this book, we will refer to Her as Our Goddess, The Lady Divine, The Mother, or the Heavenly Mother. In general, we speak of God, Our Father, or Heavenly Father and we do not consider to addressing Him with a name. Therefore, I shall treat the female aspect of The Divine with the same nomenclature as the male.

The Kabbalah

The Kabbalah is an ancient religious system of teaching that combines Jewish theology, philosophy, science, magick, and mysticism. The word 'Kabbalah' is Hebrew for "that which is received" referring to the knowledge of and inspired by The Divine. The Kabbalah teaches the practical comprehension of the upper worlds and allows the living to apply it to our immediate existence, thus attaining spiritual perfection.

This form of spiritual study allows the practitioner to take control over one's own life and transcend the limitations of time and space. "That which is received" is meant to unite humankind with The Divine. By logical understanding coupled with spiritual enlightenment, the concept of "to know God is to be God" can be achieved. Followers of the Kabbalah believe that one cannot properly function in this world without the knowledge of the upper world.

The mystical system of the Kabbalah is unique in that it speaks to each person differently. Like an onion, it has many layers. To peel one layer back in understanding is to reveal continuing layers of untouched spiritual concepts. Some students of esoteric thought take the depth of the Kabbalah to the point that it becomes an obsession. Others cannot get a conceptual foothold on the vast information that continues to reveal itself deeper and deeper, as the practitioner delves into the many layers of the philosophies of the components of God.

Many who study the Kabbalah only see the topical information of the ten spheres. Some Rabbis believe that if the name and meaning of the spheres are the only information the Kabbalah gives you, then that is the only level of understanding the Divine wishes you to have. A true Kabballist will not pass judgment on another individual's spiritual learning capacity.

Each of the ten spheres represents a specific quality or characteristic of The Divine. Many refer to these ten spheres as the ten faces of God. This is an extension of the Trinity concept, being the three faces of the Divine. Each of these spheres in turn represents characteristics of humankind. If you think logically and arbitrarily about yourself as you move through the spheres, you can apply their meaning to your own being.

We find the ten spheres of the Tree of Life placed on three columns, known to us in Kabballistic terms as the Three Pillars. They are from left to right, the black pillar (female), the gold pillar (both male and female), and the white pillar (male).

At the top of the Tree of Life is the sphere of Kether; this is the Crown of the Tree of Life. It is in this sphere that the limitless, genderless Creator without form dwells, and as a result is very difficult to fathom. The Godname for this sphere is Eheieh. We can apply this to ourselves by asking "how Godlike am I in my behavior? - How close am I to making the perfect example of the all encompassing Creator?" This is a status that as humans, we cannot realistically achieve, but as spiritualists we should know that it is the goal we should strive toward.

The top sphere on the black pillar is Binah; this is the sphere of Understanding. The Godname of this sphere is Elohim. Kabballist believe that this is the Great Mother, positioned on the top of the female pillar, with understanding as its primary function. As spiritualists, we can apply this to ourselves by asking, "How understanding and how nurturing am I? - How can I best reflect the compassionate aspects of the Creator and be a better example with the actions in my life?" The understanding you gain from the Binah sphere is hidden spiritual knowledge that is attainable to all of us. If you let your heart and soul search and find the answers, your mind will quickly follow and you can begin to build a solid foundation towards knowing The Divine.

The next sphere on the white pillar is Chokmah; this is the sphere of Wisdom. Kabballists have acknowledged this sphere, as it bears the name YHWH or Yahweh/Jehovah. Analyzing its position on the male pillar and the concept of wisdom, we realize this is the sphere of the Father, the male principle of The Divine. We can apply the concept of this sphere to ourselves by constantly seeking knowledge to be closer to The Divine. We can also apply this by asking, "how can I best use my wisdom? - How can I best use the wisdom of the understanding I gain from the Binah sphere?" We know that we cannot ever fully understand the Wisdom of the Creator, as long as we are on this earth. This wisdom is intended for us not to strive to *be* The Divine but instead to be more *like* The Divine.

At this point, we reach the break in the Tree of Life represented by the "invisible" sphere Da'ath. This is also referred to as Abyss, or the Rainbow Bridge, the point in which we fall from the Divine in the Garden of Eden. This sphere is represented on the Middle Pillar because both Adam and Eve (a male and a female) fell from grace. We can contemplate the Da'ath sphere by asking ourselves "am I in good graces with The Divine and what can I do to correct it? - Do I have adequate knowledge of The Divine? Do I really have knowledge of good and evil?" To get to this place of knowledge, one needs to ask, "How can I best spend time in prayer, meditation and contemplation to make myself more like the Divine?" One cannot adequately represent the Divine without first having peace within his own heart. Kabbalahists believe that their peace and path of understanding is essential to "knowing the Divine."

The next seven spheres are all personality-oriented. As the Kabbalah is the Ten Faces of the Divine, these personalities also apply to us in the same way. They are characteristics of The Divine and subsequently, the characteristics of all humankind.

The next sphere on the black pillar is Geburah, this is the sphere dealing with the Strength of Fear and Severity; it bears the Godname Elohim Gibor. This sphere deals with the "righting of wrong" aspects of The Divine: this sphere is not about judgment, punishment, or retribution but about restoring the conditions for cosmic corrections in the most expedient manner necessary.

The next sphere on the white pillar is Chesed, the sphere of Mercy and Compassion. The Godname affiliated with this sphere is El, which means "God," specifically the word "The" in a Deity context. It is also used as a suffix "el," for example in the word angel meaning, "bright shining one." This sphere presents God the Father as the provider for all humankind, translated very close to "God the Giver."

The sphere of Tiphereth falls next on the Tree of Life on the Middle or Gold Pillar, meaning Beauty and Balance. It indicates both male and female characteristics; the Godname for this sphere is Eloah va Da'ath. This name loosely translates as "the God-Goddess of Knowledge." This sphere symbolizes Jesus, however the genderless position of the Tree of Life depicts the male-female beauty and balance of Christ. The Tiphereth sphere is literally the child of the Binah and the Chokmah spheres. Jesus was the human embodiment of celestial understanding and wisdom; the planetary Sun (Son) association with this sphere also encourages the child principle of the Divine.

The sphere Hod positioned at the bottom of the Black pillar, indicating female aspects, and meaning Glory and Honor. The Godname associated with this sphere is Elohim Sabbaoth, which does not translate well to modern English, but a close attempt would be "the God-Goddesses of everyone."

The sphere Hod is usually coupled with the sphere Netzach. It is positioned on the White pillar, indicating male aspects, which means Victory and Achievement. The reason for the coupling of these spheres is the Godname for Netzach is YHWH Sabbaoth, which translates as "the God of Hosts." Together these spheres work as conductors of The Divine's love and grace to humans, for which all souls contain.

The sphere of Yesod is positioned on the gold pillar, indicating both male and female characteristics; the meaning of this sphere is The Foundation. The Godname associated with this sphere is Shaddai el Chai, which translates most comprehendible into "the Almighty Living God." The aspects of this sphere revolve around the spiritual source of our reproductive capabilities; its planetary association is the moon as it correlates to feminine monthly cycles, birth cycles, and the cycles of life. When one begins to path walk the Tree of Life, this sphere represents the foundation that must be laid initially. This sphere is the beginning of accessing the subconscious mind and the intuitive concepts that brings all us of closer to the Divine.

The last sphere is Malkuth. It is very multifaceted and means The Kingdom or God's presence both these being on Earth. The Godname affiliated with this sphere is Adonai, which means Lord. The presence of God on the Earth is what denotes the affiliation of the Shekinah to this sphere (a feminine form of God dwelling on the Earth). However, Malkuth is on the gold pillar not because the Shekinah is both male and female but because She affects all of humankind, both male and female. This female affiliation of God come to Earth gives this sphere many possible interpretations.

The affiliation of Malkuth being the bride of the Tiphereth (Jesus), for some gives the interpretation as being the Church, the figurative bride of Christ; while others see this female aspect as the companion of the Tiphereth (Jesus) being Mary Magdalene; and for some it gives the mother position on Earth as being the Virgin Mary. Yet, others see this sphere as the celestial mother of the Tiphereth (Jesus), being the Spirit of God in the Old Testament, or the Holy Spirit in the New Testament.

The four elements are also associated with the Malkuth Sphere. Many consider the elements to be a lower form of angels. The elements of earth, air, fire and water are instrumental to the concepts of Wicca and are the building blocks of all creation.

The Tree of Life is mentioned briefly in Genesis 2:9 as the forbidden tree of knowledge, of which Adam and Eve should not eat; however, in the Kabbalah, the Tree of Life is profiled to explain the very existence and composition of The Divine. The Tree of Knowledge is also compiled of complex mathematical formulas that are without errors and loopholes. The underlying theme is the concept of each letter of the Hebrew alphabet possessing a definite deeper meaning of life and the mysteries of the universe. It is comprised of ten spheres known as the sephiroth. There are actually eleven spheres counting the invisible sphere of Da'ath. Twenty-two lines or paths symbolic of the twenty-two letters of the Hebrew alphabet interconnect the sephiroth. Together the 22 paths and the 10 spheres make up the "32 Paths of Wisdom."

Due to the complex nature of the Kabbalah, Hebrew males were forbidden to study this mystical work until the age of 40. It is believed that studying the Kabbalah earlier in life would have serious mental repercussions; the vessel, which Kabballist call the human body and receiving mind, is not mentally ready to comprehend the depth of the Tree of Life.

Gnosticism

After the crucifixion and the resurrection of Jesus Christ, there were many sects of Christianity. This is very different from today's denominations in that the sects differed on the actual framework of Christianity, and modern denominations differ only on the point of views within a standard framework. The Councils of Nicea I (325 A.C.E.), Constantinople I (381 A.C.E.), Ephesus (431 A.C.E.), and Chalecedon (451 A.C.E.) determined this framework.

To sum up the problems of the Early Christians, one could say that there was absolutely nothing "organized" about organized religion. The sects of early Christianity fought within themselves and like modern Christians, each group professed to know "the single truth" concerning Jesus, salvation, and the wrath of the Old Testament God. A force of arms decided the contents of the Holy Bible that we read today and the Gnostics were the group that lost. As a result, little was known about Gnostic Christianity until the Nag Hammadi Library was discovered in 1947.

The views of the Gnostics were drastically different from the other sects; their approach to Christianity was mystical and eclectic. They called the Christian Deity the "One True God." They viewed this God as having a feminine part, which was the Spirit. They believed that Jesus was the celestial offspring who came from the union of the Male God and the Female Spirit to form the Holy Trinity.

The concept of the Demiurge is another point that separated the Gnostics from the Orthodox Christians. Demiurge is the name that the Gnostics gave to the Old Testament God, who can be noted for His vengeance and wrath. The Gnostics did not believe that this was "the Good Father" or the "True Father" of whom Jesus preached.

Another large difference between the Gnostics and the Orthodox Christians was the creation myths. Before the creation of the Earth, the Gnostic Goddess Sophia accidentally gave birth to the Demiurge. Sophia's name comes from the Greek word for "wisdom," the personification of the Female Divine.

There are various versions of Her myth. According to one, Sophia is the active creative force and Her consort is the passive creative force. The male aspect of the Divine is the Unknown but Good God and the Heavenly Father of Jesus. The story goes that Sophia desires to have a child God, but she does not "actively mate" with the Good Father in a fashion that we might envision. However, Her thoughts become manifest by accident, after all She Is a Goddess! Her thought to have a child is infused with Heavenly Light and brings this Child God into being.

The exact means by which this cosmic birth process occurred was and continues to be the subject of much debate among the Gnostic Christians. According to this version of creation, Sophia's desire somehow veiled infinity, casting a shadow of heavenly matter, which lacked spirit. Therefore, the Old Testament God was jealous and not pure. The Demiurge, called Yaldabaoth, emerged from Sophia like a bad reflection or a bad dream about Heaven. To the Gnostics, the Demiurge was a parody of the true, Hidden God.

Embarrassed at Her own actions, Sophia then threw the jealous and revolting Godform out of Heaven. After seeing the results, Sophia banished Yaldabaoth from Heaven and gave it independent existence. She did not want the other Aeons (or immortal beings) in Heaven to see Her mistake. Sophia then enters into a cloud and begins to cry for all eternity at Her foolish mistake.

The Gnostics called the Old Testament God Yaldabaoth, which means "child, pass through to here" or by the name Samael, which means the *"blind god"* or *"the God of the blind."* This type of "blindness" corresponds with the Spiritual Mysteries hidden within each of us. This Godform was the arrogant creator-god of the Old Testament. In his arrogance, he spoke of no other Gods - due to His ignorance, He did not even recognize his own Mother Sophia.

In Gnosticism, the Demiurge, creator of the material world, was not God but the Archon, or chief of the lowest order of spirits or aeons. According to the Gnostics, the Demiurge was able to endow man only with psyche, sensuous soul; only the True God could add the pneuma, or the rational soul. This is the "feminine aspect of the Spirit" - the Greek term pneuma, often associated with the Holy Spirit of the New Testament. The Gnostics identified the Demiurge with the Jehovah of the Hebrews. In philosophy, the term is used to denote a Divine Being that is the builder of the universe rather than its creator.

Some Gnostics taught that the world is ruled by evil archons, among them being the deity of the Old Testament, who hold captive the spirit of humanity. They believe that this is the *true Satan*, the Hebrew "ha-satan" or adversary of the True God or the Good Father.

In the Demiurge's own arrogance and ignorance, He creates the visible world but begins to withhold knowledge from humanity. This example is made when Adam and Eve are instructed to not eat from the "Tree of Life" and the knowledge of good and evil. At this point, humankind becomes aware of themselves, their own ideas, their own opinions and begins to question the "only God they know." Thus, the anger of the Old Testament God begins and His vengeful tactics of ruling the earth is well documented.

Whether you choose to agree with this concept is up to you ... however, it does explain alot about the difference in the Vengeful Old Testament God and the God of Love that Jesus proclaimed in the New Testament.

The Gnostics even disagreed with the Orthodox Christians about who Jesus really was and what was his true purpose on earth. For the Gnostics, Jesus did not come from the Demiurge but instead had come from the True Father God and the Holy Spirit Mother. In fact, Jesus came to the earth to correct the spiritual mistakes of the Demiurge and change the path of humanity towards a peaceful form of spirituality

The Gnostics believed that Jesus taught through secret knowledge, which he did not teach the masses. The special knowledge was known as "gnosis." Gnosis was not a logical type of knowledge as one might gain in the study of the empirical sciences or by reading books. Instead, this intuitive knowledge would come from the study of our own soul or inner being through methods of meditation.

The Gnostics also disagreed on the point that man was sinful by nature, but believed in human error due to spiritual ignorance. By gnosis, they believed that the world could correct its erring ways and gain salvation. The Gnostics believed that there were many "secret teachings" that each follower could only receive directly from Christ. Like the Kabballists, these teachings were revealed once when one had made his/her vessel pure and clean to receive such enlightenment.

The Gnostics were the more literary of the early Christian sects, proven when one single jar contained 52 of the Nag Hammadi manuscripts. Included in these writings were additional gospels by the other eight disciples, additional books of Acts of the Apostles as told from the other ten apostles, the apocalypses of Moses, the Virgin Mary, and the fragmented Gospel of Mary Magdalene. In addition, infancy gospels were found pertaining to the early life of Christ, as well as the infancy of the Virgin Mary.

Most importantly, the Nag Hammadi Library contained "secret" gospels, in which Christ appeared to His disciples one by one. Christ instructed these secret revelations to not surface to the masses until after each disciple's death.

These writings proclaim a completely good God; they describe a transcendent God so filled with enlightenment and so vast that it is too incomprehensible to properly define. They speak of not only a Christian Goddess, but also several Female Deities, similar to the Pagan pantheons of Gods and Goddesses. The Gnostics believed that God was not just a being from another realm, but that each of us possessed part of the vastness of The Great Deity inside ourselves.

Similarities of the Kabballists and the Gnostics

The Gnostics and the Kabballists share similar goals of spiritual enlightenment and share the theories of Divine knowledge by Divine revelation. They each were seekers of the truth and the answers to the religious paradoxical questions of life. There are 5 basic questions addressed by the Kabballists and the Gnostics:

1. Why does the world possess both good and evil characteristics when the world was created by a God who is all good?
2. Why does this world have limits when a God who knows no limits created it?
3. Why does humankind possess characteristics of both good and evil when God who is all good created humankind and all of humankind is made in God's image?
4. Why does humankind have limits when a God who knows no limits created humankind?
5. If the very nature of God, who is limitless, infinite, genderless, without form, all good and all-knowing to seemingly be unknowable, then how is it possible for humankind to even pretend to know God?

Wicca

Wicca is the modern form of an earth-based spirituality that pre-dates Christianity. This religion is indigenous to Europe with similar life-reaffirming spiritualities all over the world; it is both new and old. Wiccans experience the Divine as immanent, as embodied in the universe, the world in all its aspects and in humanity. Followers of the Wiccan path perceive all life and all forms of life to be sacred.

Modern Wicca incorporates ancient ways and modern liturgy in their practices and rituals. This is easy to see if you realize that the structure of Catholic Mass is Christianized rituals of the Old Religion. As a compromise, the Roman Church incorporated customary spiritual paths into Catholicism in exchange for accepting the Christian male Trinity. The Church Christianized all the major holidays or "holy days" of the Old Ways in order to pull these cultures under the reign of Rome.

Other compromises came into effect when Pagan gods and goddesses were made Saints, and the Catholic Church turned seasonal observances, known as sabbats, into special ceremonial masses. When one is given the option of death or merging one's own spiritual belief system with Catholicism ... well, history documents the outcome!

Wiccans believe that by attuning themselves to the natural rhythms of the earth and the universe, they can be one with nature, and ultimately experience communion with the Divine on a personal level. The Jewish Mystics as well as the Native Americans also practiced this type of attuning. Wiccans honor nature as the ultimate spiritual teacher and they contemplate wisdom inherent in the seasonal cycles of the earth.

Wiccans, like Native Americans and other indigenous groups, lived close to the earth. They planted and harvested crops by natures' own signs and the changing of the seasons. They respected their relationship to nature as sacred, because this is all they had to live by and direct their life. Their food, clothes, housing and medicines were all taken directly from the earth.

Wicca is a non-dogmatic religion. There is no *'Wiccan Bible'*, religious scriptures, or prophet. Instead, children learned an oral tradition by spoken word from their parents and grandparents. Wiccans follow the seasons (the Wheel of the Year) and follow the cycles of the sun and moon for planting, harvesting, gathering healing herbs, as well as their ritual observances giving thanks, praising and communing with The Divine.

Wicca is a system of techniques, dealing with spiritual insight achieved through living in harmony with nature; the mastery of which enables each individual to experience the Divine personally.

A basic Wiccan concept is that each individual has the capacity to experience the sacred mysteries of life that gives life true meaning. The Divine is experienced in prayer, meditation, ritual, and working with the development of psychism of which all humans are capable. However, unlike many modern religions, Wiccans feel the presence of the Divine in all aspects of their lives such as growing a garden, preparing a meal, working and providing for their families. The Divine is present in the Wheel of Life for each individual: choosing their spiritual path, falling in love, building a family, giving birth, and growing old. Wiccans feel The Divine presence in the air they breathe, the water they drink, and the food they eat. Wiccans respect the Earth as sacred, as it nourishes and sustains human life as well as all the planet's creatures and plants.

Wiccans have one fundamental ethical precept: "An' it harm none, do what ye wilt." This honors the great freedom that each individual has the right to ascertain truth, to experience The Divine directly, and to determine how to best live her or his own life. With that freedom, however, comes a profound responsibility that none may be harmed by one's choices and actions. Harm includes not merely physical actions, but harsh words, aggressive and confrontational behavior that would cause mental or psychic stress, thus being harmful.

As with all religions, individual Wiccans may reach different conclusions when applying these fundamental concepts to modern problems. Political or moral issues such, as vegetarianism, abortion, or participation in war is an individual choice as are the perceived karmic repercussions, or the lack thereof.

Wiccan spiritual practices, often referred to as "magick," are in fact ancient techniques for changing ones own consciousness at will in order to better understand and commune with the Divine. Wiccans coming from a Christian background may understand "magick" as an answered prayer, or a miracle. Any action perceived to be Divine after a spell, ritual, or prayer can be considered magick.

The primary purpose of these Wiccan techniques is the transformation of oneself to be closer to the God and Goddess. Developing the gifts from the Divine is a necessity to Wiccans; it is important to use the gifts to one's full capacity in order to live a moral, ethical, joyous, and spiritual life. They also use these techniques for practical ends such as healing, divination, purification, blessing, and the raising of energy to achieve positive life goals. Some of these techniques, which may include prayer, meditation, ritual, drumming, singing, chanting, dancing, and journeying require wisdom, maturity, patience, passion, and an abiding commitment to the sacred.

Spellcasting is one of the most misunderstood aspects of Wicca. It is NOT a means of having power over people or nature by the use of supernatural forces. Spellcasting is actually a form of ritual and meditation which is very similar to prayer in other religions, except that, instead of beseeching the aid or intervention of an external deity, the indwelling Divine energy is drawn outward into the world through harmonious interaction with the Divine presence within. The idea of controlling others and having dominion over nature is alien to Wicca; Wiccans do not work with diabolic or supernatural powers nor do they seek to have power over others.

Wiccans do not actually believe in a "devil" or Satan, only the absence of good; they believe each person has the capacity within him or herself to be wholly good and spiritual, to strive for Oneness with the Divine. If a Wiccan chooses to do less than moral or ethical things, they do not blame it on Satan or any demonic supernatural forces, because each practitioner has the freedom of choice and freewill to live a positive or negative lifestyle. In other words, you do not hear a Wiccan claiming "the Devil made me do it."

The essence of Wiccan spirituality is respect for and attunement with the natural energies of the earth and the universe. This attuning one's self with the Divine is each practitioner's personal goal. It is unethical to engage in any form of spiritual work that seeks to control, manipulate, or have power over others. While work may be done on behalf of another, such as healing which is an important and ancient aspect of Wicca, even this is never done without the knowledge and consent of the person who is being assisted.

There are many different traditions (similar to denominations) within the Old Religion. Some reflect the particular practices of certain ethnic groups such as Celtic, Norse, Welsh, Greek, Italian, Finno-Ugric, and Lithuanian. Some are part of the initiatory traditions made public by such practitioners as Gerald Gardner of the Gardnerian Tradition and Alexander Saunders of the Alexandrian Tradition. Still other traditions practice with the guidance of published works and draw positive aspects from many traditions.

Some Wiccans work alone and are called solitaires; they search within themselves for inspiration and practice in solitude. They work alone either by choice or due to the lack of like-minded Wiccan groups in their area. Some practitioners work in a mutually agreed upon group structure. Many groups include men and women, however there are some men only and women only groups.

Some followers of the Wiccan way are strong believers in spell casting or "prayers with props", while others are not interested in that aspect at all but instead favor the simplicity of the religion and its peaceful fulfillment. Some pagan traditions that Wiccans observe may date back for thousands of years, while others have only been around for only a few years.

Now looking in retrospect, we can see the common underlying themes and similarities between these three mystical belief systems: Wicca, Gnosticism, and Kabbalah. All three religions believe that meditation and psychic connection is the true way to commune with The Divine. One could conclude that the beliefs system of all these religions postulates that the true "Oneness" of the human spirit with the Divine can *not* be obtained by merely reading the ancient texts over and over. Taking on the love and adoration of the Saviour Jesus, the spiritual warmth of the Mother Spirit, and the respect of the Father God is also needed to become one with the Divine. At this point, I can easily see where the occult philosopher and Kabballist Dion Fortune defined the Great Law: "All Gods are the Same God and All Goddesses are the same Goddess."

Frequently Asked Questions

How Can Christianity and Wicca Mix? How can that be? Isn't being a Christian and a Wiccan oxymoron? The term Wiccan does not automatically indicate "anti-Christian" - this is the single most misunderstood concept revolving around Christian Wicca. This is a stereotypical way of thinking and a spiritual prejudice. As the researcher and author, obviously I have been able to draw the parallels of communing with the Holy Trinity within the spiritual framework of Wicca. However, the numbers of people who have claimed to study both Christianity and Wicca, and have not seen the parallels have overwhelmed me.

To be very honest, I am not the original person to set about Christianizing the practices and sacred Days of Power of The Wicca, Pagan religions, or any earth-based religions. As much as I would like to take credit for this - the Roman Catholic Church did this first. The Catholics are truly in many aspects the original Christian Wiccans or ChristoPagans!

Understandingly, it is human nature for us to not see the obvious truths standing directly before us. The change that the truth brings about in one's own life is a scary thing. It is much simpler to be spiritually ignorant to esoteric concepts rather than to complicate one's mind and soul with unfamiliar ideologies. The modern Church tends to frown upon anything outside beyond the mundane.

Most people don't consider the many sects and denominations of Christianity as being oxymoronic; they are merely different approaches. For example, when a Christian worships as Baptist is that an oxymoron? No, of course it is not! When a Christian worships as a Catholic or a Protestant, we don't consider this an oxymoron; we consider this a difference in theory and practice within the umbrella of Christianity.

Likewise, Wiccans identify themselves by tradition. Some of the traditions include Dianic Wiccans, Gardnerian Wiccans, Faerie Wiccans, Celtic Wiccans, and Eclectic Wiccans. What is wrong with considering Christian to be another tradition of Wicca?

Spiritual labels such as Dianic, Baptist, Eclectic and Catholic only define the technique of worship the practitioner uses to commune with the Divine. This concept is the same as when a Christian worships as a Wiccan. If it helps you to think of Wicca as another denomination of Christianity in order to better understand this spiritual path for yourself or to explain to others, then by all means, feel free to present it in such a light.

So, what aspects make Christian Wicca not an oxymoron? Below, I have tried to list the most frequently asked questions and address the most commonly distorted concepts revolving around practicing Christianity in the framework of Wicca.

Question 1: How is it possible for a Christian to worship as a Wiccan? Wiccan ceremonies are not set up with an absolute Deity(s) system. Instead, Wicca is set up so that any pantheon of Gods and Goddesses can be acknowledged. Wicca allows the practitioner to worship the male and female aspect of The All in an understandable and personal way regardless of any religious, ethnic, or spiritual background. You may find that many books denote the male and female aspect of the Creator Spirit as merely the God and the Goddess. Wicca is best defined as a general worship format in which the practitioner supplies the Deity or Deities of their own belief system into this spiritual path.

Most Pagans tend to accept the fact that Jesus was a great teacher and healer. His parables and ideas were peaceful and filled with messages of love and goodwill for our fellow human beings. It is the distortion of Christ's teachings and the misuse of the power of Organized Christianity that bothers Modern Pagans. This book has come about because it bothers eclectic Christians as well! Christians who accept the Mother aspect of the Godhead share the bitterness of misogyny with Neo-Pagans and share the common distaste for the financial and political arena that modern religion represents.

Question 2: Doesn't the Bible speak out against so-called "witches" and other forms of divination? Perhaps, but only in the literal sense of the word, and literal, symbolic and figurative contexts of the Bible have always been its point of controversy. However, if the words of the Bible have been thrown out of context due to the reality of passing through the hands of morally and ethically corrupt humans in position of power, then one's own personal research and conclusions are only means of gaining spiritual responsibility and peace of mind.

The most widely abused verse of the Bible against Wicca comes from Exodus 22:18: "Thou shalt not suffer the witch to live." That sounds straightforward until you realize that the English word for witch is the Hebrew term *kasheph*, most often translated as "a poisoner." Researchers believe this use of the word came about during the King James administration when the royal family's paranoia ran high. They feared assassination from within due to poisoning and they relied on food and drink testers. *Kasheph* also denotes the characteristics of a greedy, selfish, or immoral person. It often implies one who will do willful harm. In Exodus 22:18, it was an aggressive use bordering on assassination or indirectly calculated ways of murder. As words and phrases are prone to generational changes, vernacular use, or slang, one may feel this is the case here. It is for this very reason that Latin is used in legal and medical terminology; it is a dead language and is not subject to changes in phraseology.

Question 3: Wiccan rituals are not like typical church service; is this type of worship wrong for a Christian? This specific question always comes from Protestants because open-minded Catholics will look at a Christian Wicca Sabbat and say, "this is very much like a mass"!

Actually, there is a very sound reason for that: Christianity spread worldwide via the Roman Catholic Church. Their tactic for converting Paganism into Christianity was to make the rituals of Pagans into masses, make each set of Pagan Deities into Saints, in exchange for taking on the Christian Triune God; those opposed or those who did not conform were killed. The Sword or the Lord - its your choice. This method of absorbing the earth-based religions was a very simple but highly effective plan.

If you are a Protestant, you must remember that you are a split-off of the Roman Catholic Church. You are the religious affiliation that protested the Roman Catholic Church. If you are a Roman Catholic, then all your masses and ceremonies are based on or stolen directly from the Pagan religions.

Another reason it may seem unfamiliar is because the average Christian church service is lead by a single minister or priest and the congregation is generally passive. Here is a good time to speak out on behalf of the "hands-on" benefits of personal spiritual participation involved in Wicca. This aspect allows each individual to be their own minister and to be their own congregation at the same time. Each person is a priest and each person is a priestess. In Wicca, each practitioner can have a part to play in the worship service. Whether you practice Wicca alone as a solitary or worship with a group, the assembling of the ceremony is part of the learning experience. Once parts are established and assigned, then the practitioner has to "do his/her homework" to be prepared for the ritual. This tends to enhance your knowledge of the ceremony, cause heartfelt emotions toward the rite being conducted, and as a result, deepen each practitioner's connection to the Divine.

Practitioners gain so much more spiritually by getting involved with the entire Circle of Worship than by merely listening to another person recites passages from a book. Regarding this aspect of methods of worship, I often compare the Organized Church to going to college - at some point you have to put down the books and begin to put your education into use. No one can make a living being a professional college student! (Trust me, I know people who tried!) Would you trust a surgeon to operate on you if she/he has only studied the human body from a textbook? Wicca encourages the Christian to take the lessons of the Bible, put them into action and to write their own ceremonies. Then just do it - celebrate your Communing with the Trinity!

Question 4: Should a Christian perform spells of magick? Let me clarify that spells can best be interpreted as "prayers with props"; these props may be candles, incense, healing herbs and oils, as well as the "not yet" defined powers and properties of semi-precious stones and gems. The use of candle magick continues in the Catholic Church in the forms of Novena candles. When Catholics call upon Saints in this fashion, it is no doubt a similar practice akin to magick. However, the Roman Catholic Church would not agree to terminology. Their pseudo-magical practices are more fashionably referred to as "popular religiosity." There is absolutely nothing different about this practice from forms of candle worship in Wicca. Both are points of focus in one's meditations, the only difference is that Wicca does not fall under the rule of the Vatican.

Question 5: How can a Christian observe Pagan sabbats such as Yule, Mabon, Ostara, Samhain, Imbolg, Lughnasadh, Beltane, and Mid Summer? This answer is very simple. You already are doing this, if you celebrate any of the holidays. Many if not most of the holidays and Saints' days in Christianity, especially in the United States, derive from Pagan (or pre-Christian) holy days.

The Roman Catholic Church Christianized the Pagan holiday of Yule into Christmas, as it is the time for all Young Gods to be born according to thousands of years of Pagan traditions. Mabon is Thanksgiving. Ostara is Easter. Samhain is Halloween. Imbolg is Candlemas or Groundhog's Day. Beltane is May Day and is a time for many spring celebrations with the dance of the May Pole and the crowning of the May Queen. Midsummer, the lesser sabbat of the summer equinox, seemed to need an association of some kind, so the Catholic Church re-associated this observance as John the Baptist Day.

The date of Christmas was the celebration of the return of the sun ("the light of the world") and the birth of the Solar God, the "sun god" which was parleyed into the Son of God by the Organized Church. In almost every ancient religion, the young God was born at the winter solstice, and Christianity is no exception. While, it was widely recognized that Jesus might have been born in the late summer and recent re-evaluations point to early April, the Roman Catholic Church chose to continue the Pagan Young God birth cycle as a winter holiday.

Easter, once known as Ostara, is the time for procreation. Therefore, gifts of rabbits and hunting eggs continued to be a very common celebration. Ostara, the Spring or Vernal Equinox, which was a symbol of fertility as well as the origin of the Easter Bunny (a highly procreative species) in hopes of bringing bountiful crops. The Hebrew celebration of Passover actually began as a fertility festival as well.

Question 6: What is the difference between a Circle and a Coven? This is a two-fold question. Just as many Wiccans are steering clear of the term "witch", many are steering clear of the term "coven." Due to the negative light that the Inquisition, fundamental Christianity and society in general has put on the words, many Wiccans of all traditions are opting to avoid these terms that carry alot of false information and prejudice. Slander and spiritual hatred is never attractive.

A Circle is often a group of solitary practitioners of varying beliefs who gather to celebrate Esbats, Sabbats, and special healing or prosperity rituals with total respect to each other's personal beliefs and views of The Divine. Usually this type of eclectic Circle or a group of Wiccans of various traditions does not have an appointed Priest or Priestess. Instead, there is usually a group facilitator of the rituals; he/she organizes which parts each person is going to take in the ceremony. For example, someone is appointed to cast the protective circle, one is appointed to call the quadrants, one is appointed to invoke The Divine Spirit, and others are appointed for coning the power towards the goal of the ritual, as well as the other components of the ceremony.

A Coven is a more organized group. There is usually only one tradition observed among all members of the Coven, and the belief structure is very similar, if not nearly identical between the practitioners. In addition, there is usually a hierarchy of leaders within the Sacred Space. Christians should be able to understand this as having a Pastor, Elders and Deacons, or Priests, Ministers, Lay Ministers, Reverends, Stewards, Music Directors, and Youth Leaders. This is the same for Wiccan Covens.

Covens and Circles can be all male, all female or both male and female. This is a personal choice of each group regardless of being a Coven or a Circle. Many groups feel that male and female personal energies do not work together when raising the cone of power towards a particular goal; other groups feel no problems in mixing personal energies of the two sexes. Sometimes there are problems of mismatched energies in any Circle and Coven, regardless of it the group of practitioners are the same-sex or mixed. Often, not everyone's goals and intentions are the same; some have a less positive outlook on life and this can affect the entire group.

Question 7: How can a Christian use the pentacle and not the Cross of Calvary as a sign of their religious affiliation? Today, it is hard for Christians to believe that the cross was not always the symbol of

Christianity. Originally, the cross was non-existent in the Early Church because it was considered in violation of the second commandment and considered a "graven image." To the sensitive Christians of the early church, Jesus on the cross was a grim memory. The cross was a cruel execution device used in ancient Rome. The cross has also been used worldwide as a religious symbol, even in cultures that had no contact with Christianity such as many aboriginal tribes in Africa.

In antiquity, the solar cross, or the equal arms cross resembling a "plus sign", was used by the Knight Templars, the Celts, followers of Janus/Bacchus, and Hebrew mystics. It represented the equal male and female energies of the universe - the Goddess and the God. The vertical line represents the male aspect of the Divine and the horizontal line represents the female aspect of the Divine.

Through out history, we find the pentacle on jars of food and in ancient homes as a sign of protection from evil. Likewise, it is an adornment symbolizing protection and unity through the all-encompassing One Spirit. We shall discuss more details about the real meaning of the symbol of the pentacle later in this book.

Many Christian Wiccans choose to wear their cross *in addition* to their pentacle to promote the idea that Trinitarians are Wiccans, too. In addition, it serves as a statement of affirmations for Christians who are putting the Goddess back into the Trinity. Other ChristoWiccans simply wear a pentacle and find no reason for anyone to question that their choice of God and Goddess is any less credible than those of other Wiccan traditions are.

Question 8: How does the Trinity fit into Trinitarian Wicca? The Trinity concept is not exclusively Pagan, however it does pre-date Christianity. Trinities have been part of almost all the world religions since the beginning of recorded history. Until Christianity appeared on the scene in the early first three centuries A.C.E., all trinities were female. The female trinity is the three aspects of the Goddess: the Maiden, the Mother, and the Crone (or the Wise Woman). As women were the bearer of children, the bringers of life - the female role in most cultures was more respected that after the onset of Christianity. At this time, each family was lead by a matriarch; the eldest living woman was the matriarch of each family, and her words of wisdom were highly respected.

One aspect of the Trinity often not mentioned or celebrated, as strongly among Wiccans is the Triple Male Concept. This Trinity is the Son, the Father, and the Sage (or the Wise Man). For the most part, I believe from first hand experience that Christians who turned wholey Pagan often put stronger emphasis on the Triple Female Concept of The Divine than longtime Wiccans, seeming as some form of mental, spiritual and psychological cleansing of the jealous and bitter Old Testament God who projected the message of "worship me or die". Indeed, this is not a very loving concept. If it is spiritual love that is missing from one's own religious practices, then the rebellion of the vengeful Christian God is an understandable human reaction.

Staying with the Trinity approach to the worship of the Godhead was an intelligent move. However, Christianity realized the Trinity in the form of Triple Male Godhead composed of the Father, the Son, and the Holy Spirit. Before the Gutenberg press and the release of the King James Version of the Holy Bible, it was very common to find that the newly absorbed Pagans-turned-Christians would honor the Christian Holy Trinity of male deities completely in addition to their regional or cultural Goddess from their specific earth-based religion. Ironically, no one in the masses even questioned the gender of the Holy Spirit except for scholars and those who would not readily fall under the brutalities and persecutions of the Roman Catholic Church or the Inquisitions.

Question 9: Are there other Christianized Pagan and Catholic tie-ins that are still in practice? Yes! Many of the 'traditions' in church and in the modern world are not those derived either from the Bible or from the letters of the early church fathers. Instead, they derive either in whole or in part from Pagan rituals or from the secular rituals of Pagan cultures.

For example, the advent wreath is part Christian, part Pagan. The evergreen wreath, the use of candles and increasing numbers of them, and its circular shape are all derived from various Pagan solstice rites, but the current number of candles (four), their arrangement (a cross), and their colors (purple and white, and sometimes a lighter purple or pink one) derive from Christian symbolism. A Pagan solstice wreath would have candles in the elemental colors, or all one color, probably red, to symbolize the new birth of the sun.

There are two candles on the altar of Catholic Churches used for illumination; many realize this is a parallel to the God and Goddess candles of Pagan Altars. In addition, votive candles used during mass derive from Mithra worship. The candles represent the Sun. In almost every religion in the world observes a God and Goddess. In other spiritual paths, equal male and female aspects of the Divine are revered because humankind is both male and female. Most equate God with the sun. It is for this reason that candles are usually the focal point of the Male aspect of God or the young Solar God, which is Jesus in Christianity.

Question 10: How do angels and saints integrate into Christian Wicca? The Roman Catholic Church has worked with angels and saints for two thousand years. They work as guardians, guides, protectors, and celestial intercessors between humankind and the Divine. Many of the saints were Pagan Gods and Goddesses absorbed into the Catholic Church.

Many Christian Wiccans likewise feel a spiritual connection to deities of the Old Religion as they are appropriately referred to as Patron Gods and Goddesses. The do not supercede the Holy Trinity; they are simply compliment the Father, the Mother, and the Holy Son.

The Goddess Brigid was one of the most difficult transformations in religious history and yet, Sainte Brigit is the most famous of the Pagan Goddesses turned Sainte. There was reasonable amount of conformity as the Irish people took on the robe of the Roman Catholic Church as they embraced the teachings of the Father, the Son, and the Holy Spirit. However, these people refused to give up their beloved Brigid. Unable to eradicate all elements of some Pagan religions and fearing to loose all of the Irish Tradition, the Roman Catholic Church made Brigid a Sainte, renamed with the Christian approach as Ste. Brigit. For all the Pagans who missed their beloved Kernunnos, whose symbol was the Stag; the Catholic Church replaces Him with Saint Hubert and Saint Tatheus. Sainte Ann proved to be a replacement for the Pagan Goddess Ana or Dana.

Pentacles:
Dispelling the Myths

"Men never do evil so completely and
Cheerfully as when they do it from
Religious conviction."
Blaise Pascal, Penses (1670)

The superstition revolving around Wicca's affiliation with the use of pentacles is overwhelming, given our modern technological age and the simplicity of the facts commonly associated with this symbol. Today, society wrongfully views the five-pointed star within the circle as evil, regardless of its position upright or inverted. Eliphas Levi was the nineteenth century esoteric philosopher and occultist, who first differentiated between the good and evil aspects of the pentagram.

The pentacle is "the Star of Life." It has a known history of over 8,000 years, and is the one symbol for Spirit. It has stood the test of time and it is in almost ever society in the world, in both the east and the west. Approximately 3,500 primarily rulers of Kingdoms (B.C.E.) used the pentacle in Ancient Mesopotamia as a military symbol. The pentacle indicated their earthly political power and military achievements that reached to the four corners of the known world.

The Pythagorean mystics considered its geometric qualities to be the symbol of perfection, both mathematically and metaphysically, of absolute perfection. Pythagoras believed that the number 5 is the sum of the feminine element "two" and the masculine element "three." Thus, the five-pointed star reinforces the numerical belief that humankind symbolizes the Creative Union of masculine and feminine aspects of the Divine.

The pentacle was a common symbol, and often worn amulet, that signified protection and healing in Babylon. The Early Greeks called this symbol *pentalpha*, the birth-letter or alpha, the first letter of the alphabet, interlaced five times, meaning "life" or "health". Today, Wiccans use the pentacle for focus in rituals and wear it for protection in the form of jewelry. It does not stand for anything evil; it merely stands for the five elements or the five building blocks of all creation that you see around you.

In the physical world, the elements are earth, air, fire, and water. The top point of the star represents the key element of the spiritual world, which is the Great Spirit, the One, and the Divine. In terms of the relationship of humanity to the relationship of The Divine, the five-pointed star represents humankind or the microcosm and the perfect circle depicts The Divine or the macrocosm. Again, in essence, we are all "little gods and little goddesses." In other words, we are made of the Divine and the Divine reigns within us as much as in the celestial realms.

Among the Hebrews, the pentacle was a symbol of "the law" and truth. It also corresponds with the five books of the Pentateuch, the first five books of the Holy Bible and The Torah. Depending on your sources for information, the five-point star is the Seal of Solomon, because King Solomon inscribed it on his magick ring. Some religious historians dispute its direct affiliation with King Solomon totally, while others believe that it was developed and used in conjunction with the hexagram.

The early philosophers and students of rationality, held the five points of the star to also represent the five senses, through which earthly knowledge enters the mind. The center can stand for the sixth sense, the deep unconscious, or the ethereal connection of each human being with the All (the High God) or the Higher Self.

For the Druids, the pentacle was a symbol of Godhead. In Egypt, it was a symbol of the 'underground womb' and bore a symbolic relationship to the concept of the pyramid form. During the Inquisition, the Old Religion and its symbols went underground, in fear of the Church's persecution, and there it stayed, gradually withering for centuries.

Until Medieval times, the early Christians affiliated the Pentacle or "The Blazing Star" as the representation of the 5 wounds of Jesus Christ's during the crucifixion: the crown of thorns, the whips to his back, the hands, the feet, and finally the spear that pierced His side. It carried no evil implications at this time and many Christians found that it was more symbolic of the Savior.

Without doubt, most people have seen Leonardo's advanced sketch "The Microcosmic Man" depicting the body posed within the star position. Many centuries later, the sketch also defined the muscle structure of the human body; though everyone immediately see the star figure of a man inside a perfect circle. Leonardo's advance was far from a name commonly associated with pentacles and witchcrafts of any sort.

The next series of events surrounding the pentacle is very ironic for the Modern Christian Church. Although newly converted to Christianity, the Roman Emperor Constantine still was regarding himself as a god in his own right. He chose to use the pentagram on his seal and amulet. Everyone in the empire used the pentacle regardless of their religious beliefs. Ironically, when the newly founded Church of Rome needed a symbol, it was Constantine's elderly mother, Helena, who chose the "True Cross," to replace the ancient pentacle. She allegedly discovered this religious article during her travels in the Holy Lands. She is recorded as finding the actual cross that crucified Jesus, in a cave presumed to be the burial tomb and site of the resurrection.

After reporting her religious findings to Constantine, the True Cross was taken to Jerusalem and placed in the Church of the Holy Sepulcher. It remained there until 614 A.C.E. when Chrosroes II of Persia captured Jerusalem and moved the cross to his homeland where it remained for thirteen years. At this point, the Roman Emperor Heraclius defeated Chrosroes and reclaimed the cross, first placing it in Constantinople and finally taking it back to Jerusalem. It is believed to have been placed in hiding there by the Christians in 1009 C.E., where it remained until the First Crusade in 1099. The Christians possessed the True Cross until 1187, when Moslem leader Saladin captured it. Despite all the needless deaths during the Crusades attempting to reclaim this relic, no trace of the relic is believed to exist today.

It seems that everyone accepted the use of the torture device of the cross as the symbol of Jesus Christ. I have often wondered if guillotines or a lynching had been the form of Christ's death sentence - would Christians be wearing little gallows or nooses around their necks. Few followers of Christ seem to stop and realize that the Romans were who crucified Jesus in the first place and then later decided to deify the Saviour. So, of course, the Romans wished to do away with all forms of pre-Roman religion, because earth-based spiritual paths were not profit-oriented religions and they were merely a pebble in the shoe of the Orthodox Christianity.

The pentacle had no 'evil' connotations before the time of the Holy Inquisition. Rather its simplistic design implied celestial truth and understanding, religious mysticism and the work of The Creator. However, during the long period of the Holy Inquisition, there was no limit to the cultivation of lies and accusations in the 'interests' of orthodoxy and elimination of heresy.

For the first time in history, the pentagram, a folk-symbol of security and dedication of their faith to The Divine, was equated with 'evil'. Thanks to the Holy Inquisition, the pentacle was given a bad reputation and the underlying truth behind its meaning has unfairly taken a hard beating over the years. The meaning of this pure symbol of life and protection has been distorted and perverted for centuries. To the uneducated, it is as a symbol of evil, a form of satanic worship, and the league of all aspects of the paranormal that is dark and sinister.

The disinformation revolving around the meaning of the pentagram still exists in our society today. The Church launched into a long period of the very diabolism it sought to oppose. The Inquisition took Eliphas Levi's drawings of good and evil depicted through the pentacle and connected its symbology to a the Horned Hunter or the God of the Hunt - who represented the hunter-gather aspect of men who provided meat for their family for winter. The God of the Hunt had antlers depicting a stag deer. These antlers quickly became horns and perpetuated the Orthodox concept of Satan or "the devil."

The duty of the Holy Roman Inquisition was to destroy all forms of worship and spiritual symbols that did not align perfectly with the Roman Catholic Church. This included the destruction of the recognition of the Goddess and the "Star of Life." While, as a Christian, you may not be a practicing Catholic and may be of another part of the Protestant movement, if you accept these teachings of disinformation and continue the procreation of hate, lies, and superstitions against the earth-based religions ... then you might as well be part of the Catholic Church's Inquisition yourself. You are continuing the religious persecution.

"The Star of Life" took its most recent blow to reputation in 1966, when Anton Szandor LaVey adopted the inverted pentagram as the official symbol of The Church of Satan. Many students of esoterica realize that LaVey was much more a showman and seeking of the spotlight than a spiritual leader. He used shocking ideas and practices profiling the deification of the anti-Christ. LaVey received plenty of free publicity due to his Circus antics and media-oriented approach to taboo spirituality and sensationalism.

However, more often than not, teenagers will wear an inverted pentagram as a rebellious act against their parents and society, simply for the shock factor, or to impress their peers. These acts simply have to do with drawing attention to one and rarely deals with any true form of religion - especially Satanism.

Unfortunately, most religious fundamentalists of all faiths misunderstand all this information. Instead of trying to educate themselves to the true meaning of the 5-pointed star, they take word of mouth from the superstitions passed down by the Holy Inquisition. What is surprising is that well educated Christians of all faiths will not take the time to educate themselves about the history of the pentacle, but instead find it easier to just ignorantly cast stones. The teachings of the Living Jesus tell us to not pass judgment on others, yet Fundamental Christians will do this very thing! Jesus' teachings spoke out primarily against hypocrites, not sinners as the Modern Church does. Instead, organized religion breeds and encourages hypocrisy by lashing out at other churches and condemning others to "hell" without listening to the hypocritical words the Church is proclaiming.

Trinitarians: Father, Mother, and Son
The Three are One - Who Is The Mother?

Trinitarianism is the common belief system and perception among most Christian sects concerning the doctrine of the Trinity, or the Triune God. Of Trinitarianism itself, some people ask, "how could three be equal to one?" Using a simple mathematical equation to explain this seeming paradox of the trinity, at first we would most commonly think of $1+1+1=3$, not 1! However, we really could explain the One Spirit as $1 \times 1 \times 1 = 1$.

Although the Trinity contains three equal units with distinguished properties, they unite in essence and form a Oneness without any of the units losing any individual identities. Thus, each personality's work and function manifest in forms of compartmentalization so that humankind can better comprehend the Divine.

The Trinitarian Tradition is the proper tradition for Wiccans of the Christian faith to acknowledge themselves. A Trinitarian Wiccan believes in the Triune God, represented in the aspect of God the Father, God the Son, and God the Mother. In mainstream Christianity, the feminine aspect of the Divine does not exist. The concept of the Goddess wears a mask in Christianity; She appears as a dove or a golden ray of light. She is referred to as "Wisdom," "the Glory of God," and the "Spirit of God." Quietly and neatly, the Divine She was swept under the rug and is all but absent from the current version of the Bible.

It is now during this century's spiritual awakening that the Goddess is emerging and re-claiming her rightful place in the Holy Trinity. William G. Gray quotes the following about the Lady Divine in his book "Qabalistic Concepts":

> "Apart from a dove, many artists indicate the Holy Spirit
> as "living flames" or radiances and beams of light.
> They dared not show a feminine element in any portrayal
> of the triple Deity.
> Officially, for Semites and Christians alike, woman was
> An afterthought of God, who created her as a "helpmate,"
> for Adam's benefit.
> Besides, it was Eve who got poor old Adam
> flung out of Paradise."

William G. Gray also goes on to make a humorous but sadly true comment about the feelings of the Jewish Priest and Fathers of the Hebrew religion at the time of translation. Gray states "Jewish men prayed to God daily and thanked Him for not making man in the image of a camel or a woman - the two most contrary beasts of the desert!"

In Hebrew, The Holy Spirit is the *Ruach ha-Kodesh*, which is a feminine gendered term. However, when translated to English, The Spirit of God or The Holy Spirit has no gender acknowledgement. Throughout, the Bible depicts The Holy Spirit as a dove or a golden ray of heavenly light.

The Bible veils the Mother God, and has for almost two thousand years; the books where She is plainly present, have been removed from the canonized Bible and declared heresy. The council members are the ones who made the Trinity into a Triple Male; the fact because the Roman Catholic Church was downplaying the female aspect of God, previously observed by all earth-oriented religions worldwide. Patriarchal dominance in the Christian Church runs so deeply in Modern Christianity that Christians cannot even conceive the idea of a Mother-God.

Matriarchal societies and families became patriarchal almost overnight with the onset of the politics of the Catholic Church. An example of the extremities of the early Orthodox Church is the fact that the Christians of this era had their doubts about the ability of the salvation of the souls of women. The early Christian Church actually voted to decide whether women had souls or not; the women won by one vote!

The worship and adoration of the Goddess was equated with the Pagan and earth-based religions. Without annihilation of the Goddess, Christianity would be simply another Mother-God religion and that would not carry the political punch that the newly manufactured Triple Male concept would. It is the common thoughts of many Christian Wiccans and Goddess-inclusive Christians that the Roman Catholic Church was not about religion and spirituality at all. The Organized Church was designed to control the masses and world politics; they did this by reaching them through their most vulnerable areas - their souls!

Several female personalities have appeared between the Hebraic to Gnostic times giving a credible claim to the title of the Christian Goddess. For all practical purposes, Mary has been the Goddess of Christendom for approximately 2000 years. While Mary is not considered a Goddess in name, She functions in the same way as the ancient goddesses. She is the Divine symbol of the holiness of womanhood. Therefore, Catholic-influenced Christian Wiccans will naturally recognize the Virgin Mary as Goddess, as she was the earthly manifestation of the female Deity.

It is interesting to note that the converted Pagans at Ephesus, the home of the Temple of Diana, refused to accept the loss of the Divine Mother. So as a substitution, the Council of Ephesus in 431 A.C.E., decreed that the Roman Catholic Church bestow the royal title of *Theotokos* upon Mary, meaning "Mother of God," however she was never considered "God the Mother" and the consort of "God the Father." Again, in 1968, the Virgin Mary was elevated in the hierarchy of the Catholic Church. Mary was declared the *Mater Ecclesiae* or Mother of the Church; subsequently she became the *causa efficiens* of Redemption. Since 1968, the Blessed Virgin Mary has become the intercessor between humankind and God; she has become the Redemptress or Redemptrix and no one can receive the grace of the Father except through Mary.

It is also important to note that many attribute Mary as the Christianization of the Basque Moon Goddess named "Mari," who also ruled the sun, the stars, and the waters of the earth. Mari was the embodiment of the most feminine Deity; her symbolism credited her as being the Mother of all living things ... a title also given to Eve, Sophia, the Shekinah, and the Holy Spirit over the Judeo-Christian timetable.

The Kabbalahists rationalize the names EHIH/Eheieh and Elohim as the One Spirit, the female and male principles of the Divine respectively. There is also the need to recognize the singular feminine name Eloah, Elat, and the Aramaic form Eloi which are derivatives of the plural name of Elohim, meaning "gods."

Often Binah, the name of the third sphere of understanding on the Kaballistic Tree of Life, is addressed as a Goddess by this name. In "The Grimoires of Lady Sheba," she invokes the Moon Goddess: "Ea Binah, Ge! Isis unveiled, hear my plea! Shaddai, El Chai Ea, Binah Ge!" The sephiroth, or sphere, of Binah is "The Supernal Mother" who takes the raw directionless energy of the second sphere, Chokmah or the Supernal Father, and gives it form and manifestation. She is considered the Bright Mother, Aima (nourishing) and the Dark Mother, Ama (constricting).

Kaballists view the Shekinah as the female aspect of the Godhead and literally translates as *"the indwelling of God."* Shekinah is delivered as more of a title than a name and resides in the Malkuth sphere, on the Tree of Life. For Kabbalah influenced Wiccans, the Triple Goddess arises based on the three Mother Letters of the Hebrew Alphabet, Aleph, Mem, and Shin.

The Gnostic Christians provide us with the Goddess Sophia. The feminine term *sophia* is the Greek word for wisdom. The word Gnostic comes from the Greek word *gnosis*, which means knowledge. This time of knowledge comes not by study or from written scriptures, but through meditation and personal revelation by the Divine; this form of spiritual knowledge differs from person to person.

In many mystic Christian formats of worship, Hagia Sophia is the acknowledged Christian Goddess; She is Holy Wisdom, and the Shekinah of the Presence. She is the Lady Divine and communes with us as the imminent breath of Life or the Divine, on the wind of the most holy; therefore, She is the Holy Spirit.

Yet others look to the "Goddess in the Gospels," Mary Magdalene as the continuation of the followers of Asherah, a daughter of Zion. The alabaster jar associated with Mary Magdalene and the washing of Jesus' feet was part of the tradition of the women who kept the Temple of Asherah. Many believe that the Magdala was the wife of Jesus and co-Messiah or co-redemntrix with Him. Many attribute the earthly manifestation of Sophia to Mary Magdalene. Whether or not she was the wife of Jesus, the Gnostic Gospels definitely refer to her as the Companion of Jesus. There is also information that there was possibly a female child, after their unpublicized wedding.

The Canaanite Goddess Asherah or "Asherah of the Seas" is a primary Hebrew Goddess. Other versions of her name include Astoreth, Astarte, Anat, and Inanna. Some early Goddess historians refer to Asherah as the Shekinah, but without a doubt, she bears the title as the Queen of Heaven, who is mentioned in Jeremiah. Asherah was the Goddess once worshipped by the Children of Israel as the wife of their God, Yahweh.

Many people become confused at the nature of the Female Divine because She is represented in many forms, both the ethereal and worldly. Some of the expressions of the Goddess include the Divine Manifestation in human form (Mary Magdalene), Supernal Mother symbolism (Sophia, Elohim, Asherah the Shekinah), and Divine Motherhood bestowed upon a human woman (the Virgin Mary). However, it is enough for now to simply understand that The Holy Spirit has somewhat become the "catch-all" personification for the feminine aspect of The Divine.

Anyone studying Judaism and the Hebrew religions and the Holy Scriptures, such as the Kabbalah, Torah, and Talmud, should recognize the term *ruach ha-kodesh* as Hebrew for the Holy Spirit. *Ruach* means "breath" or "spirit," and *ha-kodesh* are words which loosely translate to "holy." In the Old Testament, when the phrase "Spirit of God" is used, it is always the feminine Hebrew term, *ruach ha-kodesh*.

Robert M Grant, theologian and noted author of *The White Goddess*, concentrated his work on Early Christian writings, especially of the second century. In the preface of *The Other Bible*, Grant compares the androgynous nature of the Gnostic Creator God to the mystical Judaism of the Zohar, the classical work of the Kabbalah: "Yahweh is called the Father and Elohim the Mother." In this example, Dion Fortune's theory of The Great Law applies to the Christian Goddesses as well: "All Gods are the Same God and All Goddesses are the Same Goddess."

Some Christians find their Goddess by feeling and going where their heart takes them, making a move on blind faith. On the other hand, some are obsessed with a degree of proof, details, finding the clues and pieces of the missing Goddess puzzle in the Kabbalah, the non-canonized books, the Missing Books of Eden, the Nag Hammadi Library, as well as in the history and politics of the era. Both paths are perfectly acceptable. Some Christian Wiccans are more Old Testament-oriented, others New Testament-oriented, Gnostically or Kabbalistically-oriented…but are all seeking the "somewhat secretive" female aspect of The High Spirit.

Many Christians refuse to consider Mary Magdalene a possible aspect of the Goddess, yet she was Jesus' most beloved disciple, and she is the woman who followed Him all the days of her life. Mary Magdalene did as Jesus instructed and set about to tell the world of the Good News of the Saviour. Historians believe that Mary Magdalene spread the Gospel of Jesus Christ further from the Holy Lands than any of the other disciples. Often known as The Magdala, Mary made major impressions on the area now known as France. There are more statues and monuments indicating her service and ministry of Jesus found in the pre-Gaul area than in any other country in the world.

The Gnostic Gospels repeatedly speak of the disciples being jealous when Jesus would kiss her on the mouth! Perhaps this is the reason the term "Goddess of the Gospels" associates with Mary Magdalene. The Gospel of Philip says, "As for Wisdom [Sophia] who is called 'the barren,' She is the Mother of the Angels. In addition, the companion of the Saviour is Mary Magdalene. But, Christ loved her more than all the disciples and used to kiss her often on the mouth. The rest of the disciples were offended by it and expressed disapproval. They said to Him, 'Why do you love her more than all of us?' The Saviour said 'why do I not love you like her? When a blind man and one who sees are both together in darkness, they are no different from one another. When the light comes, then he who sees will see the light, and he who is blind will remain in darkness.'"

The Christian Goddess is not just about the possible deification of the Blessed Virgin Mary, or the possible deification of the companion Mary Magdalene; it is not about the assigning the title of avatar to them. The concept of the Christian Goddess is about the greater Female Aspect of God, and the many shapes and forms that She can take, just as God the Father takes many forms in our lives. This is a commonly accepted aspect of angels, who appear in all types of forms to people of this earth; I see no reason that the Divine Masculine and the Divine Feminine cannot manifest themselves in any appearance desired.

Most Christian Wiccans or Goddess Christians of any spiritual path, come together on similar views of the Supernal Mother. One post on the Christian Wicca e-list stated:

> *"I view both Mary the Mother and Mary Magdalene*
> *as incarnate aspects of Divine Feminine [or] the*
> *Shekinah. [Our worship group] uses the YHVH four part*
> *godhead a lot ... within the four parts, there is*
> *God the Mother, Shekinah in whom we find*
> *the Holy Spirit or Sophia, Magdalene is viewed*
> *as the physical embodiment of the Spirit Daughter.*
> *Currently, I see Mary as the Mother of Christ as*
> *an incarnation or avatar of Shekinah, the Mother*
> *Creator who is the mated to the Father Creator;*
> *Their offspring being the Divine Son.*
> *Therefore, we have God the Father, Goddess the Mother,*
> *the Divine Son and Spirit Daughter*
> *making up the Godhead."*

The Quadrinity has been a viable concept as often as the Trinity especially when one looks at the Jewish and Kaballistic Roots. Many view the Letters of YHWH (Yod He` Vau He`) as being representative and corresponding of many things such as the elements of earth, air, fire and water and of the Father, Mother, Son, and Daughter (notice that both the Mother and Daughter are represented by the Hebrew Letter He`). A common Hebrew point of humor among the scholars is that the Letter *"he`"* means *"she!"*

There are a couple of remote Goddesses, both Hebrew and Gnostic, with whom some Trinitarian Wiccans may identify or acknowledge in their rituals. The Hebrew Goddess Jarah, who according to celebrated Pagan author Edain McCoy in her book *Lady of the Night*, "is a Goddess of the new Moon who is seen as the bride of the Sun. She was the prototype for the Shekinah, the feminine half of the Jewish God, honored to this day, but not worshipped, by Jews as the Sabbath Queen. She was once the Sun Goddess, with the moon being a masculine figure in early Semitic mythology. Jarah was originally a masculine deity."

Edain McCoy also lists Levannah, the Canaanite-Hebraic Goddess. She was a "Moon Goddess similar to the early Hebrew Jarah, and to the Jewish Shekinah, in that she was viewed as fully one-half of the Creative Divine." Next, this brings me to mention Inanna, who was a Sumerian Moon Goddess, later called Ishtar. Some Trinitarian Wiccans wish to include Inanna in the Hebrew Pantheon. Yet, others see Inanna as purely Pagan, and of course, is one of the names included in the Charge of the Goddess, as per the Gardnerian Tradition. Perhaps, if nowhere else - Christian and Pagan Wiccans can find middle ground and common respect for a mutual Goddess in Inanna. This would be a positive step in uniting Wiccans of either side.

One Hebrew Goddess who has always been of great dispute is the legendary Lilith. Over the millennia, She symbolizes feminine independence, hatred, admiration, and fear; this is no doubt the basis of her infamy. According to the Zohar, Lilith is Adam's first wife, who refused to accept a subservient role. Lilith is the Siamese twin sister of Adam. At the time of creation, they were connected back to back. According to the Zohar, the bones of the spinal column are said to be a reminder that Lilith was actually "sawed" away from Adam. She demanded equality with Adam because they *both* had been equally created from the dust of the ground.

Lilith has taken the position as a pseudo-patron Sainte among modern feminists. They have begun to reevaluate the myth of Lilith, because she would not allow Adam to oppress her. Due to society's outlook on women at that time, she consequently gained the reputation as a beautiful demon of sexual prowess, to put it kindly. It is also believed that Lilith destroys children because God took away her children. However, psychologically, this is not a sound theory. Lilith would most likely empathize with the mothers who lose their children, not cause their loss.

Ironically, Lilith was deified in Ur, Abraham's original home. There, she was considered a great Goddess, not a demon, and not a destroyer of children. It was Christianity of the Middle Ages which focused heavily on her demonic nature. This is approximately at the same time that the Roman Catholics were having problems with women being accused of demonic practices, witchcraft, the Inquisition, and the over-deification of Mary among the "common people."

Because all human parents can nurture as well as chastise, it was common for Gods and Goddesses of the Ancient worlds to be viewed as having a dark and a light side; these two sides to the whole were often personified as "twins." The Hebrew were no exception. Many believe that Lilith was the dark aspect of the Shekinah. Parallels drawn between Lilith and the Shekinah are similar to the ones drawn between Nephthys and Isis, and Ereshkigal and Inanna.

The Gnostic Christians also acknowledged a "High Goddess" of sorts in the form of a female Aeon named Barbelo, whom Jesus spoke of in the Secret Gospel of John, as the "womb of the Universe." Jesus also calls her the first thought of the Unknowable God, and the first knowable Deity. Excerpts from the Secret Gospel of John are as follows:

"For the Perfect One beholds itself in the light
surrounding it. This is the spring of the water of life
that gives forth all the worlds of every kind.
The Perfect One gazes upon its image, sees it in the
Spring of the spirit, and falls in love with the luminous

> *water. This is the*
> *spring of pure, luminous water surrounding the*
> *Perfect One ...*
> *"Its Thought became active, and she who appeared*
> *in the presence of the Father in shining light came forth.*
> *She is the first power: she preceded everything, and*
> *came forth from the Father's mind as the*
> *Forethought of all. [Barbelo] is the first Thought, the*
> *image of the Spirit. She became the universal womb,*
> *for She precedes everything."*

Other names intertwine in Gnosticism regarding the Goddess: Throughout Gnostic literature, Sophia is the most prominent. However, other female aspects of the One True Spirit of Creation are named as Zoë, Psyche, Achamoth, Pronoia, and Epinoia.

Just because the medieval translators of the Old Testament made the Godhead a Trinity, as well as wholly male, does not mean that you can not re-educate yourself to see the sexual biases and the politics of the times that rested in the hands of the very powerful few. This is not about feminine equality but cosmic balance in the Godhead. When we read that God made "Man in his own image," many Christians find it easy to think of God creating Adam in his own image and Eve as an afterthought; but this is not what the scriptures teach. Genesis 1:27 says, "God created man in his own image, in the image of God he created him; Male and female he created them." Thus, the image of God is not solely male, but both male and female, separately and collectively. Thus, we may know that men and women are equally the image of God. Perhaps humankind is the correct term we should use, suggesting that men and women together make up the image of The Divine.

Finding Your Personal Christian Goddess

Unlike other traditions of Wicca, the Goddess or Goddesses of the Trinitarian tradition is not firmly established. Since She is not part of modern fundamental Christianity and the Trinitarian tradition is new to Wicca, many newcomers will have questions about identifying with a Goddess, perhaps by name - and there may be some confusion about "which one is the right one" and "can we accept more than one Goddess?"

Recovering the forgotten Goddess back into the original Holy Trinity may be difficult for some Wiccans coming from an extremely dogmatic Christian background; liberal Christians will have fewer problems in recognizing their personal Goddess. Here is a meditation ritual that can help you determine the name and aspects of the Female Divine who speaks to your heart and soul.

Nine is the number of the Goddess in all forms of magickal numerology, and there are many examples. The number nine is a sacred number, representing the triple Goddess three times over. Using the number 9, assemble the nine white candles (or the candle color of your choice) on a table or the floor in a position that you can sit comfortably with them and meditate for at least 45 minutes (5 minutes per Goddess candle). Imagine an invisible pentacle placed at the nexus of an invisible cross on your altar for magickal workspace. Place 4 candles at the cardinal points of the cross and the 5 candles at the 5 points of the pentacle.

Assemble your ritual at a time when you have privacy and can focus on your goal. Dim the lights. Eliminate all unnecessary sounds and distractions, such as the phone ringing, pets, or children. Light your favorite incense and allow yourself to relax and center your personal energies. You will need paper and ink to write your petition to the different Goddesses. If you wish, use dove's blood ink and a white quill on parchment paper or in your personal Book of Light.

Assign one of the names of the Christian Goddesses to each candle. The most common nine Hebraic-Gnostic Goddesses are the Holy Spirit, the Shekinah, the Virgin Mary, Sophia, Asherah, Levannah, Inanna, Elohim, and Mary Magdalene. Also, consider the Binah sphere of the Tree of Life for its namesake, Aima, Barbelo, Eloi, Jarah, Lilith, Zoë, Psyche, Achamoth, Pronoia, and Epinoia.

Inscribe the Goddess' name on the side of the candle. Anoint each candle with your favorite oil and arrange them at the nine points.

Cast a circle around yourself and call the quadrants. Light all of the candles saying the name of the Goddess to yourself as you go. Start at the top candle and hold your hand over each candle. Speak aloud what each name symbolizes to you. Be as lengthy as you wish, explaining out-loud what each Goddess means to you. You may wish to write these meanings as you go.

When you are finished with your explanations and petition, move your hands over each of the candles. Be careful not to burn your hands, but feel for special energy coming from one particular candle more than the others. Also, watch for a flame to burn uniquely or pop aloud to get your attention if you choose to use nine female figurine candles. These subtle sensations and visions will ultimately draw your attention to one particular candle more than the others will.

You will probably enter into the Goddess seeking ritual with a pre-conceived choice of the Lady and this exercise will help you to confirm your choice. It is also important to realize that just as many see the male aspect of the Divine as Jesus on earth and the Father God in Heaven, you may discover the Goddess has more than one face to you. Just as the Female Divine appears as the Maiden, the Mother, and the Crone in Pagan traditions, the Christian Goddess may speak to you in multiple ways as well.

Try not to rush the ritual or put unnecessary pressure on yourself to connect with the Goddess. Once you start to look for the Goddess, trust me, She will reveal Herself to you. After all, She has been with you since the beginning; you only had to open your eyes to find Her blessed presence!

What is the Book of Shadows?

The Key to Hidden Knowledge - is it Wrong to be a Seeker?

Before we discuss the Book of Light, I would like to explain a few points about the Book of Shadows used by traditional Wiccans. The Book of Shadows is a handwritten spiritual journal that each practitioner keeps. The word "shadows" seems to be what makes the average non-metaphysical person recoil and let their imaginations run wild into non-existent dark affiliations. The word, "shadows" tends to make persons unschooled in esoteric spirituality feel uncomfortable. In actuality, the word "shadows" does not have any affiliation with evil, Satan, or practices of the left hand path. The term Book of Shadows is actually short for *Book of Shadows and Light*.

The phrase "shadows and light" addresses the principles of Hermetic Law and the stabilization of the polarities of the universe. These are the law of physics, metaphysics that affect our everyday lives through the balanced recognition of both male and female energies of the Divine in each practitioner's own life. These are the balances of light and dark, left and right, receptive and projective, negative and positive, female and male. Wiccans of all traditions strive for natural balance and attunement with nature and the creative forces of the universe. With balance comes order, and with order come stability, progress, and accomplishment.

Lashing out at what we do not understand has always been humanity's way. In today's world of religious competitiveness, it seems that giving negative connotations to any spiritual belief system that does not coincide with one's own, is acceptable religious etiquette. Religious, spiritual and magickal intolerance runs rampant due to the lack of comparative studies of our world's theologies.

The term shadows in this case is symbolic of the spiritual mysteries hidden within all people. There have been Christians throughout the ages that have debated that this knowledge previously hidden should remain this way. Many fundamentalists oppose the supernatural and profess that *God* does not want humankind to access these spiritual mysteries. Logically, if you have the natural inclination for mysticism, then it is not paranormal at all - but instead, quite normal.

If this were not true, the Divine would not have allowed humankind to progress; the alphabet would not have come into existence, nor mathematics and sciences. Our species would have never discovered nuclear energy by harnessing the power of the atom; we would have never entered the Space

Age. Medical Sciences would never have advanced to the level of treating terminal disease and illnesses. Modern health care would not have naturally evolved, nor would the prevention of the plagues of small pox, typhoid, diphtheria, and tuberculosis. None of these breakthrough achievements would have happened if our species had remained in technological ignorance. The problem now is the challenge for the spiritual community to advance or fall to the wayside. It is for this reason that eclectic Christians, Wiccan or not, believe that Christianity must evolve or die.

One of the simplest reasons that esoteric thought is not widely accepted is because it is difficult for some people to grasp. They do not wish to take the time for deeper spiritual meditations. However, saying that *God* does not want humankind to discover the hidden meanings of the scriptures and of spiritual knowledge is simply a lazy person putting words in the Divine's mouth!

Not all can understand the key to metaphysical communion with The Divine. Daphne Moore, author of *The Rabbi's Tarot* explains, "Jesus came to teach the quick and the dead." The quick, she explains are students seeking enlightenment and gnosis. The rest of the population is the dead - those who must learn by parables and metaphoric examples. This is one reason that Wicca is an esoteric religion. By accessing metaphysical forms of spirituality, the individual experiences higher forms of personal enlightenment. A comparative example is that all persons can go to college and commit their life to higher forms of education. However, as many of us know either personally or from family and friends, college is not for everyone. This is the same for Wicca and for any form of metaphysical spirituality.

The term *occult* is frightening to many Christians new to the areas of metaphysics. A common definition of the occult is hidden spiritual knowledge. This is positive and productive hidden knowledge, not the knowledge of evil, or the study of abilities to do evil. This is knowledge comes to you through meditation and study. There is nothing dark about any tradition of Wicca and of course, more importantly - there is nothing dark about worshipping and communing with Jesus Christ through the methods of Wicca.

Now, lets please emphasize that there are no aspects of darkness in any form of Wicca! If there are any dark aspects someone is using in Wicca - then they are not practicing true Wicca. The left hand path is the name given to the darkness associated with magick or the darker forms of spirituality. This is not Wicca! A murderer may profess Christianity, yet it simply takes common sense to discern the reality of the individual's mindset and intent.

I encourage all practitioners to study other forms of esoteric spirituality; however, do not practice these paths if they are not a form of spirituality that speaks comfortably to you. Enlightenment is the key - if it is a dark practice, it is not very enlightening, is it? Use common sense. The same goes for intelligently discussing spirituality outside of your current realm of knowledge.

People who make the claim that any religion such as Wicca is evil without spending time researching Wicca is not the type of person who will talk and think rationally about spirituality. In other words, do not cast your pearls before swine! It is sad to say that any one person cannot reach a higher spiritual level. The truth of the matter is that it is not because a person cannot reach a higher level of spirituality; it is usually because they *do not wish* to attain a higher spiritual level. Superstition, lack of education of metaphysics and distorted views of esoteric religions is often the reason for people to have a closed mind to other forms of communing with the Divine.

After two thousand years of conditioning, fundamental Christians find any spiritual experience bordering on the paranormal, even Christian, and Christ-oriented in nature, to be "evil." In many ways, after practicing the worship of Christ via the methods of Wicca, I do not believe that I could go back to just being a spectator-type Christian. I can no longer believe that "God" is in a church and an Organized Religious institution is required for me to commune with the Divine. I can no longer believe that the Divine is a more male than female deity anymore than I can believe that the opposite is true. I cannot put faith in an individual, such as a Minister or a Priest, to be the one single person sanctioned by the Divine to proclaim a spiritual message.

In the Gospel of Mark 4:22, Jesus states "Things are hidden only to be revealed at a later time." The truth of this is humankind has made great technological advances in the last 50 years, however the modern church discourages spiritual advancement. Psychic gifts, higher perception, metaphysical powers ... call these things whatever you will, but you cannot call them evil nor of the occult. These abilities, created within us, originate from the Divine; these abilities function as a means by which we can reach back to Our Creator. If the Modern Church is stifling these abilities of "talking to our God" and putting limits on the spiritual morality of using them by deeming them evil and of the occult, then the Modern Church is putting limits on the Divine Creator. Do you think this is the Divine's will for humankind?

The Book of Light

Containing the Christian
Lunar Rites and Wheel of the Year

Esbats, Sabbats, & Kyriats

"There is always light in the
darkness. I will love the light for it shows
me the way. Yet, I will endure the darkness
For it shows me the stars." ——*Og Mandino*

Trinitarian Wiccans feel a more direct communion with the Triune Spirit than the average fundamentalist Christian because they accept the female aspect of the Divine. They intensely feel the spiritual love and devotion that transforms the practitioner into enlightenment. The Light of Christ and the enlightenment of Holy Trinity (Mother, Father and Jesus) are displayed in our lives by the balances of faith, hope, and love. ChristoWiccans practice this form of enlightenment in our daily lives, not just on designated days of the week.

Wiccans of the Trinitarian Tradition keep a self-written book of prayers, ceremonies, meditations, blessings, magickal notes, and references. This spiritual journal should be a place to write notes on the uses of herbs, oils, crystals, and healing recipes. It should also be an ongoing collection of ceremonies, rituals, power thoughts, prayers, spells, magickal workings, and passages of enlightenment that have been effective for the practitioner. Just as no two people are alike, no two books will be alike and there is no set formula to follow. Just as the Traditional Wiccans call their spiritual journals a "Book of Shadows," many Trinitarians call their spiritual journals a "Book of Light." In essence, the Book of Light contains each practitioner's own practices toward ultimate enlightenment with the Holy Trinity.

Your personal Book of Light should hold information and thoughts that have made a profound impact on your heart, mind, and soul as a follower of Wicca, based on Jesus Christ, the Mother and the Father. The Book of Light should contain your own interpretations, personal beliefs, and ethics of the Trinitarian Tradition. In addition, as you progress in your spiritual scholarship, additions should reflect your newfound knowledge. Any information and practical applications of working with the angels, the saints, colors, novena magick and candles, aromas, herbs and oils, forms of homeopathic healing, gems, prayers, and spells are positive additions.

More advanced Christian practitioners may wish include detailed information about the angelic alphabet, Enochian philosophies and Keys, the Conjugations of King Solomon and the many seals of Solomon, quotes from the Dead Sea Scrolls, notes on the Kabbalah, the Gnostic Gospels, and the Hebrew and Judeo-Christian mysticisms that have influenced them.

Core Beliefs

Trinitarian Wiccans believe that their spiritual path is very personal and have made long and hard soul searching decisions to practice Wicca with the Christian Trinity. Trinitarians believe the defining characteristics of this form of Wicca can be witnessed in the love for nature, fellow human beings, and most importantly love and respect for the Lord and Lady Divine, the Holy Son and the tangible evidence of Creation, our Earth. Unlike fundamental Christianity, Trinitarians strive to make Wicca a non-judgmental form of Christian spirituality.

Christian Wiccans also believe that Jesus Christ was an Avatar: a God who came to earth in the humble body of a man; He lived to the approximate age of 33. Addressing the multitudes, teaching and preaching the gospel, He presented His lessons of Divine love, tolerance, and harmony among all people in parables. He was crucified, died and was reborn on the third day and ascended into the heavens.

Trinitarians should continue to seek spiritual knowledge, as it comes in many forms: The Bible, The Apocrypha, the Gnostic Gospels, The Kabbalah, the Pseudopigrapha, and others. Each person's own interpretation of the words of The Divine should be considered just as individual as The Divine has made each of us. Christian Wiccans should read the Dead Sea Scrolls as they are uncovered and take what is useful; each individual will find their own precious message and take it to heart, while helping to fill in the holes in the Bible, perhaps providing some much needed answers.

Epistemology is the study or theory of the nature, sources, and limits to Divine knowledge. Christian Wiccans view epistemology in this way: There is one objective truth underlying the universe. We perceive the truth by our senses, our reasoning, and through different states of consciousness.

However, this truth is different for each person, since we all have a different point of view and see things a little differently. How we see this truth creates our beliefs and this in turn determines what the facts of our existence are. We construct our reality based on these facts. Change your beliefs, and you change the facts. Change the facts, and you change your reality. We can always change our reality, because we have complete freedom as to what we believe; we have the ability to change the images at any time. We can choose to see the world in a different way. This does not change the underlying truth because it is always constant. Instead, it only changes our perception of it.

Baptism

Baptism is the symbolic act of the death of the present body, returning to the womb (the water) of the Mother Spirit and being reborn into the light of Christ. It is a spiritual purification of the body and soul, cleansing oneself of the impurities of the previous life. It is a ritual of dedication.

It is symbolic of casting off the old self and taking on a new spiritual life based on the teachings of our Lord and Saviour, Jesus Christ. Many Christians ponder the symbolism of baptism. Is it the physical water or the symbology of the rebirth through the Spirit that saves one's soul; is it a combination of the two? That is for individuals to decide for themselves.

The *Gospel of Philip* states: "Through the Holy Spirit we are indeed begotten again, but are begotten through Christ in the two. We are anointed through the Spirit. When we were begotten, we were united. None shall be able to seek Him either in water or in the mirror without light. Nor again will you be able to see the light without water or mirror. For the reason it is fitting to baptize in the two, in the light and in the water. Now the light is the chrism."

However, the *Gospel of Philip* goes on to say: "The chrism is superior to baptism, for it is from the word 'chrism that we have been called "Christians," certainly not because of the word 'baptism.' And it is because of the chrism that "the Christ" has his name." In her book, *The Gnostic Gospels*, author Elaine Pagels references the Gnostic's views on Orthodox Christianity and baptism by saying, "In protest against the majority, they insisted that baptism did not make a Christian; according to the *Gospel of Philip*, many people 'go down into the water and come up without having received anything,' and still they claim to be Christians."

Another example of the importance of baptism comes from the *Gospel of the Hebrews*, written by Jesus' earthly brother or stepbrother James. The verse reads: "And it came to pass when the Lord was come up out of the water, the whole fount of the Holy Spirit descended upon him and rested on Him and said to him: 'My Son, in all the prophets was I waiting for you that you should come and I might rest in you. For you are my first begotten Son that reigns forever.'

"Jesus answered, Verily, verily, I say unto the, except a man be born of water and of the Spirit, he cannot enter into the kingdom of God." (John 3:5)

"Then Peter said unto them, repent, and be baptized everyone of you in the name of Jesus Christ, for the remission of sins, and ye shall receive the gift of the Holy Ghost. For the promise is unto you, and to your children, and to all that are afar off, even as many as the Lord our God shall call." (Acts 2:38-39)

The ceremony of Baptism remains the same as what is normally taught as acceptable in all Christian faiths; the primary difference being the acknowledgement of the Mother Goddess, as shown in this example:

From Sinner to Saint, From Darkness into the Light
You are baptized into the Waters of Life
To be submerged once again into the Mother of All the Living
To Rise and Be Reborn to this World
To Walk in the Newness of Life
You are baptized in the name of
The Father, the Mother, and the Blessed Son, Jesus Christ
Through The Divine, all things are possible
Arise to be a living Testament for Their Namesakes.

Many Christians who choose to practice the Trinitarian tradition of Wicca have already been baptized in the church of their current and/or former faiths. Being re-baptized to worship the Holy Trinity in a Wiccan fashion is not necessary, because we are baptized into "The Father, Son, and The Holy Spirit" not into the Catholic church, the Church of the Latter Day Saints, the Baptist church, or the Methodist Church. However, if anyone wishes to be rebaptized for any personal reason, I think that is appropriate for that individual; others should respect his/her decision for renewal of re-birth as a Christian within the framework of Wicca.

Baptism is a very personal sacrament for each person. One should choose the method of baptism that makes sense in their heart, mind, and soul. Some of the more familiar methods include full immersion, sprinkling, and anointing.

The Ceremony of the Baptismal Kyriat occurs at Summer Solstice, when the Baptism of Jesus Christ by John the Baptist is honored. Ironically, the Roman Catholic Church Christianized the Mid-Summer ritual as John the Baptist Day. At this time, Wiccans of the Trinitarian tradition may wish to renew their vows of dedication and rebirth by anointing their forehead and heart area with a drop of water. This represents the reconfirmation each practitioner wishes to renew for his or her mind, heart, and soul. This water should be present on the altar. You can do this as a solitaire or as each member of the group. No Christian should scoff at any catalyst to make a practitioner excited about their faith again. Thinking things to be unscriptural is part of the dogmatic way of thinking that all Christian Wiccans should leave behind.

Beliefs of Personal Gnosis

Reincarnation
Rapture and the 7 years
The Original Sin
Why did Christ die for us?
Practicing Christian Wicca as a religion only
Practicing Christian Wicca with earth-based, folk or celestial magick
The Concept of the Demiurge
The Concept of Satan
Tools of Divination
Heaven, Purgatory, and Hell

The beliefs listed above affect all practitioners of the Christian faith, regardless of affiliation and denomination. Admittedly, these are topics of controversy. These personal beliefs are just what they are described as and we obtain these beliefs through personal revelations of hidden knowledge or *gnosis*!

The whole concept of gnosis is that each person's need for spiritual enlightenment varies. What strikes a chord of enlightenment in one person may not affect another person. Some spiritualists find communion with the Divine through the study of books, history, and politics of the ages. Some persons find the beauty of the Divine not in a book of words but in the beauty and simplicity of a flower or the laugh of a newborn baby. Others need dreams and visions to move their soul towards the realization of the Divine; others need logical proof or physical evidence to enlighten them.

The concepts listed at the beginning of this section are not part of the primary belief system for Christian Wicca. If these concepts of spiritual choice become doctrines instead of ideas, then the precepts of freewill are moot. To keep the open tradition of Wicca open, minds cannot close to trivialities of the worship service. Instead, one simply creates another Christian denomination.

Denominations automatically bring in complications and compromise within the Christian belief structure. In most denominations, free will is not a respected or encouraged aspect of spirituality. There is a structure of rules and/or laws within denominational Christianity, which gives each particular sect or worship, group its defining characteristics. There are politics within even the most minimalist protestant church with Elders and Deacons vying for decision-making powers over the congregation.

Loosing the dogmatic trappings that organized Christianity presents is the prime motivation for turning to Wicca. Christian Wicca allows the spiritual and freethinking Christian to worship the Holy Trinity as each practitioner sees fit, without having to give up the Christian Trinity in order to practice Wicca.

Reasonable Guidelines

All Trinitarians should equally honor, respect, and commune with our God, our Goddess, and Jesus. Together the male and female aspects of the Divine or The GodPair make up The Single Creative Force in our world and universe; their Blessed Only Begotten Son Jesus Christ makes the Holy Trinity complete. The Holy Trinity is the Holy Family.

The Wiccan Rede states "An' It Harm None, Do What Thou Will." The Christian Bible states a similar belief, such as Matthew 7:1 - "Judge not, lest ye be judged"; and of course, the Golden Rule: "Do unto others as you would have them do unto you." While we are all Children of the Divine, we have free will but we cast our own fate with every step we take along the road of spirituality. This is as a spiritual "cause and effect" way of thinking.

During the ceremonies, no bloodshed is required, be it human or animal. This is not part of any Wiccan or Christian ceremony. The sacrifice of Jesus' life and the shedding of His blood replace all need for animal sacrifices, such as those portrayed in the Old Testament. Again, let me reiterate and stress that blood is not required in any ceremony, ritual, prayer, or spell, in the Wiccan Religion. This is one of the most widely spread rumours of disinformation surrounding the worship system of Wicca.

Building Constructs of Rituals and Ceremonies

Esbats, Kyriats and Sabbats

The following section of the book serves as an outline of information on how to create Christianized versions of Traditional Wiccan rituals, ceremonies, as well as the purpose for each step of the rite. Variations in the details of any practitioner's ceremonies are not an indicator of a less effective ritual in any way. Instead, ceremonies are as individual as the practitioners themselves are.

Remember, the following ceremonies are not dogmatic; they are only examples. Each practitioner should tailor their rituals to best suit their spiritual needs and focus their energies on the aspects of the observance that speaks to them personally. Wicca encourages creative spirituality and there are many Christian sources for Trinitarian Wiccans from which to form the bodies of their rituals.

The following ceremonies have been written either for a solitary practitioner or for a Trinitarian Circle of worship. A solitary practitioner may wish to cut the ritual down, while Circles may wish to assign parts to specific members. The role of a priest and priestess is not necessary for a Circle, unless the Circle so desires. If no priest or priestess is appointed, then one person tends to naturally become the facilitator of the Circle. This person usually takes on the responsibility of the content of the spoken ceremony, the arrangement of the sacred temple, and appoints parts for the participating members. While all observances are as individual as a snowflake, the rituals should include some aspects of the following elements of worship.

Purification of One's Self

The self-purification bath has been traditional to many religions for thousands of years. It's purpose is to literally wash off the negative energies of the world and of the day. Daily bathing is a luxury to which our generation is accustomed, as well as the actual convenience of indoor plumbing. However, in less modern times, only very special occasions warranted a bath; for The Wicca, esbats and sabbats were definitely a special occasion. Perhaps the gist of the saying "cleanliness is next to Godliness" comes from these types of cleansing rituals.

For modern practitioners, the most effective purification bath occurs when there is no hurry or disturbances. If you are a solitary practitioner, you may wish to take the telephone off the hook; it is often a good idea to tell friends and family that you will be busy for the evening, in order to insure some private time for communing with the Divine. A very easy purification bath is simply to take a bath by candlelight. For example, I prefer using white 7-day jar candles placed about the bathroom, along with incense. Next, add salt to the bathwater and ask The Divine to bless it to the consecration and purification of one's own body, used in the same manner as Holy Water. Then if you wish, put the specific or preferred oils in the bath water that will best help you develop your mindset for the evening's ritual.

Each sabbat and esbat has corresponding oils and herbs that you may choose to add to the bath; the oils can also be used for anointing oneself. The aromas of these oils help to attune the mind and body to the upcoming ceremony. While meditating and relaxing in the self-purification bath, attunement tea is wonderful for relaxing; its flavors are also directly associated with the seasons and the celebrations.

Purification of the Worship Area

When holding a Worship Circle outdoors, there is very little need for the purification of the area. However, some may wish to cleanse the outside by the elements of earth, air, water, and fire just as you would the indoor worship circle. Traditional Wiccans often use a besom, a handmade broom used for the symbolic sweeping of negativity away from the designated sacred area. The broom never touches the ground; instead, it is a spiritual sweeping.

The Organized Church has made this benign act of symbolic cleansing into something ugly and superstitious; many Christians have made a mockery of the association between Wiccans and brooms. The traditional use of the besom has even been associated with evil. Ironically, the use of besom is symbolic of *removing evil* or dark energies from the area, with the intent for purification before the practitioners enter the natural temple.

If fundamental Christians would research Wicca before making such accusations, then there would be more spiritual respect and a greater degree of religious tolerance in the world. If a fundamental Christian finds this symbolism foolish, it might be a good thing to remember that Jesus taught in parables even during Communion. While partaking of the Lord's Supper, we are not actually breaking Christ's body and we are not actually drinking Christ's blood - this is simply another form of spiritual symbolism. It is the intent that matters.

For indoor Circles, vacuuming, mopping or sweeping is a good rule of thumb. Then before the ritual, treat both areas the same: sprinkle with holy water or consecrated salt water (which is composed of the element of water and salt from the element of earth) and follow by waving incense (which is composed of the element of fire and delivered by the element of air).

Simply sprinkle the area with the consecrated salt water. Then follow the same path by waving the incense through the air (often in the pattern of a banishing pentagram).

To consecrate your own holy water, simply add an appropriate pinch or two of salt, representing the earth, to a small bowl of water and hold it toward the sky and ask this or similar blessings:

"I call upon the Holy Trinity: We ask you to bless and
Consecrate this water and this salt for the
Elemental Purification of our Worship Circle.
Representing the Holy Mother:
Of the Earth and Water of the Sea —
So As we Will It, So Mote It Be!"

To consecrate the incense representing the element of air and the flame representing the element of fire, again speak toward the sky and ask this or similar blessings:

"I call upon the Holy Trinity: We ask you to bless and
Consecrate this flame and this incense for the
Elemental Purification of our Worship Circle.
Representing the Holy Father:
By Fire and Air - Glory to Thee
So As we Will It, So Mote It Be!"

Assembling the Altar

Assembling a Wiccan altar for Christian practitioners is not difficult, unless you place unnecessary and cumbersome requirements on yourself. A Trinitarian's altar is only a little different from the layouts of a traditional Wiccan altar or a traditional Catholic altar; actually, a hybrid of the two types of altar can be a good rule of thumb.

Like the traditional Wiccan altar, Goddess or Our Heavenly Mother goes to the left side of the altar. Following the same guidelines, God or Our Heavenly Father goes to the right hand side. However, the center of the altar is reserved for Jesus. All Trinitarian Wiccans' altars will differ because no two practitioners are alike.

The basic tenet of Wicca is that there is no wrong way to worship the Divine. As long as there is sincerity in your heart and no malice in your intent, the Divine will accept all of your efforts of worship with equal love. Therefore, any way that you wish to assemble your personal altar is correct, if you are comfortable with the choices you have made.

This theory also applies to the fact that there is no wrong way for your Worship Circle to set the altars for Esbats, Kyriats, and Sabbats. If everyone in the Circle is happy with the pre-ceremony setup of the altar, then that is all that is required. A practitioner of any faith cannot truly be in communion with the Divine if they are in an unpleasant environment. If any Christian is upset with persons around them or uncomfortable with the arrangement of the worship service, then their total focus cannot be on the Holy Trinity. This is common sense. This applies in the natural outdoor temple or in a church building made by human hands.

Articles found on the altar usually include a statue or figurine, or perhaps a novena candle as the visual representation of the Father, the Mother, and the Blessed Son. Remember, these are not idols to worship but articles of focus; they are tools for meditation and visualization.

The practitioner may place any objects on the altar which are of great personal meaning to the individual, such as a photo of a loved one or perhaps a piece of jewelry belonging to a deceased family member who is very important to you. Amulets, healing stones, charged crystals, and specific tarot cards and/or runes can enhance one's spiritual experience during the ceremony. The practitioner's Book of Light should be included as necessary articles for the altar, especially if anyone needs to access their rituals and ceremonies contained in their book.

It is a good practice for all Trinitarian Wiccans to have their Bible of choice on their altar, and incorporate passages or particular verses that they feel are associated with the ceremonial theme. There are so many words of wisdom in the Bible perfect for your ceremonies, such as those found in Psalms, Ecclesiastes, and Proverbs. In addition, the Wisdom of Solomon and Ecclesiasticus in the Apocrypha are great sources of affirmations. From the Nag Hammadi Library, the Odes of Solomon, the Psalms of Solomon, and The Thanksgiving Psalms bring newly discovered words of wisdom, which are just as effective, worthy, and useful today.

Incense is very important in any ceremony because it is another form of cleansing the sacred area. It causes clinging negative energy to be banished from one's psyche, aura, or energy field. This negative energy may come home with you from the workday or just the oppressive stress that is associated with living day to day. The Hebrew are one of the earliest recorded religions indicating the use of incense in their rituals; it was their belief that incense carried prayers upwards toward Heaven and to the Divine.

The altar should face the direction corresponding to the season of the ceremony observed. I remember the directions of the altar by word and concept association. Rituals taking place in the winter should face the direction of North, which I associate with the North Pole. I associate the

East with spring, which reflects the rising sun and the return of warmth to nature. The heat of the South can easily be remembered for summertime rituals, which leaves the opposite setting sun position of the west as the direction for the season of autumn, as the heat of the sun also diminishes.

While there are no exact rules in eclectic forms of Wicca, some basic guidelines are always helpful. For example, you may wish the Trinity Candles to be white for all ceremonies, except for Samhain, when they could be black, as a sign of solemn remembrance for those who have passed on. For Trinitarian altars, the Trinity Candles can double as the luminary candles. Traditionally, luminary candles are the main two candles usually found on both Roman Catholic and Pagan altars; they are present primarily for lighting the area before the lighting of candles with symbolic purpose during the ceremony.

Some Circles prefer to be more creative and let the ceremonial color themes carry over into the choosing of the color of the Trinity Candles as well as the altar clothes and decorations for the worship Circle. Often the simplest rule of thumb is to use the primary color of the Sabbat, Kyriat, or even work with the color patterns of the Lunar Rites that can be associated with the names of each of the Full Moons.

When we place the quadrant candles on the altar to represent the four elements instead of at the cardinal points of the Circle, we call them secondary candles. In every tradition of Wicca, the quadrant colors follow the pattern of yellow in the East, red in the South, blue in the West, and green in the North.

As Wiccans, we are all familiar with the elements of earth, air, fire, and water. However, as Christians, we should be mindful that in the making of the tabernacle, Moses was instructed by God all of its specifics. It was planned in balance with nature, the universe and in concordance with "God's will," and how the Divine should be worshipped.

In Exodus 40:22-30, the God of the Old Testament instructs Moses on how to set up an altar room, or the tabernacle, to house the Ark of the Covenant using the elemental cardinal points. I know many Wiccans and Pagans who set up an altar room in their home in a similar manner. Moses was directed to set the table on the north side of the tabernacle. Upon this table, Moses set the bread, representing the element of earth, which we can interpret as being used for the ritual of communion, similar to the ritual of cakes & wine. In Exodus 40:24, Moses sits the candlestick, representing the element of fire, on the south side of the tabernacle. Exodus 40:27, the Bible states that Moses burned sweet incense. In Exodus 40:29, the altar of burnt offerings, representing the element of air, was placed at the entrance of the tabernacle, of the east. Lastly, in Exodus 40:30, the element of water is represented with a basin of water in the west, used so that all may wash their hands and feet before entering.

Casting the Christian Circle

When the practitioner casts a circle, it is the act of creating the natural Sacred Temple. It is a circle of protective energy. When casting this protective circle, the term is misleading or at the very least inaccurate. However, it is actually casting a protective sphere of energy as it creates a dome above the worship area and equally arches underneath the circle. It is similar to the concept of a rainbow. On the ground, we only see a 90 to 180-degree arch. However, if you are in an airplane, you can see that a rainbow is actually a full circle. Likewise, just because we cannot always able to see the entire circle, does not mean it does not exist. Casting the Circle of protection is the same.

This protective energy emanates from the Divine and the building blocks of nature: earth, air, fire, and water. The sacred worship space is a non-physical temple or natural church. Wiccan temples of worship are not manmade buildings. Like the Gnostic Gospel of Thomas explains, that the Divine "is not in a building made of wood or stone; split a piece of wood and I am there, lift a stone and you will find me."

This sacred space should be revered as holy ground and given the same respect that a practitioner of any faith would give his or her own church, temple, or tabernacle. The concept of outdoor worship, when the weather permits, is the desire of being closer to the Divine. The earth is the original creation in Genesis 1:1; why worship in a building that separates the practitioner from the original creation?

Some practitioners can actually see this bluish-white protective energy, while others can only visualize it. If you have such a gift from the Divine, you will see that it clearly marks the perimeter of the Worship Circle. One can cast the Circle mentally, with the traditional Wiccan athame or wand. One can simply cast the Circle using only the index finger. The method of casting is up to the practitioner, as the goals and results are the same.

Practitioners establish the circle of protective energies in order to keep positive spiritual energies inside the worship area and to keep negative forces (or non-positive spiritual energies) outside. Casting a circle *widdershins* (counterclockwise) verses *deosil* (clockwise) is merely a matter of choice. The terms widdershins and deosil are words of antiquity, they are Anglo-Saxon in origin and part of the terms used by practitioners of the old pre-Christian religion.

The overtones of casting a circle in a particular direction are not necessarily automatically banishing or automatically empowering. It seems to vary from tradition to tradition. Ironically, with the onset of Christianity, casting a circle deosil became increasingly popular with even the Pagan religions. Because Jesus is equated with the Solar Lord or the Sun God and is called the "Sun of Righteousness" (which is *not* a misprint for "Son of Righteousness"), casting a Sacred Circle in the direction of the Sun became popular. Accompanying Christianity was the patriarchal reign and the intolerance and fear of feminine supremacy of The Mother, thus the widdershins ways were debunked through superstitions by declaring them evil.

However, astrologically looking at circle casting, the moon, which is the symbol associated with the Mother God indeed travels counterclockwise, as do all of the planets. Given this information, it is best for Christians to cast a Circle by widdershins for Esbats to further honor the Mother and to follow the path of the Moon. Likewise, it is best for Trinitarian Wiccans to cast Deosil for Sabbats and Kyriats for the Patriarchal reverence, following the male/sun relationships of the Sabbats.

The Challenge

The Challenge is part of the ceremony that is symbolic of instilling united trust and representing devotion and love among those participating members of the Circle. The mini-ceremony confirms that all practitioners are involved in the ritual because of their own freewill and they are not participating under duress. For newcomers to Wicca, especially those of a Christian background, the Challenge may seem like an unusual way to express love and trust, given the use of the athame. If working with the ceremonial blade is uncomfortable for your Circle, simply do not use it.

Remember, the beauty of ceremony and symbolism is very important to all traditions of Wicca; it is no different for Trinitarians. Do not let the Challenge of love and trust be confused with being a "threat" to worship. The pre-ritual Challenge is symbolic of the entering practitioner's freewill to choose to enter and commune with the other individuals and the Divine in perfect love and perfect trust. The key to how this differs from the Catholic takeover of the earth-based religions is that the individual has the right to walk away from the blade of spiritual decision without the consequences of death.

An appointed member or volunteer of the Circle holds the athame in a reverent and non-threatening challenge position toward the practitioners. The challenger usually asks a simple question to those who wish to enter the Circle. The statement of the Simple Challenge is usually stated and followed with the question that requires a reply. One of the most common examples of the Challenge is: "It is better to rush upon this blade (or run from this blade) than to enter the Circle with fear or hatred in your heart. How do you enter?"

One of the appropriate replies is: "In Perfect Love and Perfect Trust." Trinitarian Wiccans may wish to reply: "In the Perfect Love and Trust of the Holy Trinity" or in a reply more akin to the traditional form, such as "In Perfect Christian Love and in Perfect Christian Trust."

Practitioners entering the Circle usually line up outside of the circle and wait single file for the individual challenge at the east quadrant. Once inside the Circle, participants should find their way to their positions.

Since more and more Circles are now open and eclectic, there is not a permanent initiation ceremony or an initiate program as popularized by traditions of Wicca such as Gardnerian and Dianic. Instead, most Circles have adopted a simple challenge and response for the Wiccans participating in each particular Circle.

Anointing & Crossing Oneself upon Entrance

Anointing the practitioners with oils is very common in many religions of the world. It often represents a miniature form of rededication to the Divine and personal purification before entering the Sacred Space. Again, it is as a personal symbol of reclaimed baptism before each ritual or ceremony conducted.

As the Trinitarian tradition of Wicca is Christ oriented, Ceremonial Magick works more readily than with Pagan traditions of Wicca. The Kabballistic Cross works perfectly for anointing. Making the sign of the Cross is not the sole domain of the Catholics; instead the cross has been the symbol of protecting the heart chakra or heart cavity, wherein people once believed to be the dwelling place of the soul.

The Kabballistic Cross is made using the Solar Cross, which has equal arms vertically and horizontally, indicating the balance of the male and the female forces of the universe and of the One Spirit. The four points dictate the placement of the words "Ateh, Malkuth, ve-Geburah, ve-Gedulah; Le Olahm. Amen." This is Hebrew for "Thine is the Kingdom, the Power and the Glory Forever, Amen."

It is a very simple ritual. Touch your forehead and say, "Ah-tah", which means "For Thine...[is]"; touch the top part of your abdomen/heart area and say, "Mol-Koot, " which means "the Kingdom", touch your right shoulder and say, "Vih-G'boo-Rah", meaning "[and] the Power", and touch your left shoulder and say "Vih-G'dew-Lah" which means "[and] the Glory." Now clasp hands together like in prayer and say, "Lih-Oh-Lahm Ah-Mane," which mean "Forever, Amen."

I find special multiple meanings in the mentioning of the Hebrew word *Malkuth* (meaning "kingdom") when crossing yourself, as its word/position placement is over the heart. It coincides with the Gnostic Christian Gospel of Thomas in the concept of "the kingdom of God is within you and all around you." The Malkuth Sphere on the Tree of Life corresponds with The Shekinah, according to Kabballistic theories; this applies even more for Christians who feel the Goddess or female aspect of God in their lives. Even fundamentalists know the importance of the Holy Spirit dwelling in our hearts, more accurately in our souls.

Invitation of the Archangels, Elements, Spirits, and Keepers of the Watchtowers

The elements of earth, air, fire, and water are the building blocks of our Earth. Those four elements directly correspond with the four directions of north, east, south, and west, respectively. Many Judeo-Christian theologians feel that the elements are a form of earthly angels that rank below the position of the angels, the lowest level of beings, in the angelic heavenly hierarchy known as the nine choir. A quadrant is the term for the elements aligned with its specific direction. Many practitioners also use the term corners, (as in the four corners of the earth) or the term the quarters (as four quarters make a whole).

Beings known as the Watchers or Guardians protect each Quadrant. These Guardians act as the Keepers of the Watchtowers in most traditions of Wicca. Watchtowers simply refer to the direction of the compass, the element associated with it, as well as the meaning of what each element represents.

We affiliate the direction of east with the color of pale to mid yellow, the element of air, and the human qualities of intelligence, ideology, invention, and mental productivity. We affiliate the direction of south with the color of vibrant red, the element of fire and flame; the human qualities of this quadrant correspond to heated or strong emotions such as love, lust, and anger. Modern affiliations of this quadrant and the element of fire include the emotions and frustrations of the daily work routine. Wiccans considers all aspects of life celestial and earthly to possess male and/or female characteristics, the elements are no exception. The elements of air and fire are male in gender.

Water and earth are the female elements. They are more easily recognized as feminine, due to the symbolism of the womb, and the universal term Mother Earth. The direction of west is affiliated with the color of cool to mid blue, the element of water and the human qualities of intuition, clairvoyance, and psychic abilities. The direction of north is affiliated with color of fertile green, the element of earth, and the human qualities of mother-like nurturing and grounding. Grounding involves keeping your own energies or the energies of others mentally and spiritually stable.

Each tradition of Wicca tends to have an influence on how the practitioner perceives the Guardians. For example, Christians who are new to Wicca most commonly perceive the Watchers or Guardians as angels, archangels, and good spirits. Some Wiccans associate the Guardians with dragons; while many Celtic Wiccans find favor in fairies, pixies, and sprites.

If you choose to invoke the Guardians of the Watchtowers in the form of the archangels, then you should call them according to their affiliated quadrant. The archangel Raphael is the Guardian of the Watchtowers of the East, which is the affiliate of the element of air. The archangel Michael is the Guardian of the Watchtowers of the South, corresponding to the element of fire. The archangel Gabriel is the Guardian of the Watchtowers of the West, associated with the element of water. The archangel Uriel is the Guardian of the Watchtowers of the North, who oversees the element of earth.

Regardless of how we view the Watchers or the Guardians in our own minds, we must equate them as highly evolved beings in both mind and spirit, who have an attraction to the earth. It is important to view them with comfort as well as respect. They are present in the circle to be helpful and protective; they even seem to show signs of a good sense of humor at common ceremonial mistakes - so, never be embarrassed when things are not letter perfect during your ritual. We have a sense of humor because the Divine has a sense of humor, as well as the beings that attend the Divine!

The Quadrants are the four directional points of the sacred circle. The purpose of calling the quadrants is twofold. First, practitioners look to the quadrants for protection of the sacred space, and those in it, against unwanted spirits that may inadvertently attach themselves to the orb of power. Second, they are present in the sacred space to give wisdom and insight, guiding the participants through the meaning of the ceremony and what the ritual involves.

You make a circle on the earth plane for protection when you cast the circle. The Quadrants make a square using the elements on the celestial plane within the circle. Many practitioners who visualize the Watchtowers tend to attribute them with qualities of being approximately 17 feet high. I sometimes see them as turrets of a castle, surrounded in mist of the corresponding colors of north, east, south, and west, as a fertile green, pale yellow or off-white, a vibrant red and a light cool blue.

In the invocation of the Watchtowers, it is important to know all the characters that each quadrant represents and incorporate them appropriately into the desired outcome of the ceremony. For example, in a healing ritual, you may state: "Hail to the Arch angel Raphael, Keeper of the Watchtowers of the East, Guardian of Good Health and Celestial Healing - we invoke thee!"

Trying new invocations is encouraged because one can ever really know until they try if a new approach works for you or not. Never speak an invocation that does not seem right to you as a Christian practitioner of Wicca. Always follow your instinct and the feelings that make you feel as one with the genderless Spirit.

Invocation of the God and Goddess/the Trinity:
Prayers for Divine Presence

In traditional Wiccan circles, the word "invocation" refers to gaining audience with the quadrants and the God and Goddess. I should clarify that the word "invocation" is not a word of command or the attempt to hold powers over the angels or The Divine; instead, it is a term that indicates a hospitable and humble *invitation*. You can think of an invocation as a form of prayer that requests the presence of angels, elements, and The Divine within the Worship Circle.

If you choose to avoid the word "invocation" because it makes you uncomfortable, try using the word "invitation." For those new in the worship ways of Wicca, especially those who come from a Christian background, remember that this spiritual path is a more peaceful and personal way to worship the Holy Trinity. You are in charge of your own spiritual practice in Wicca, so if there is any aspect that makes you uncomfortable, you have the freedom to modify your worship accordingly.

The true meaning of the word "invocation," especially in regards to a Deity, is the act of drawing/inviting The Divine into you. This is very similar to what some Christian denominations call "putting on the Christ." The first century Christians devoutly believed that the divine "is inside you and all around you" as stated in the Gospel of Thomas. Traditional Wiccans also hold a similar belief in the fact that we are each little gods and goddesses.

So why invite The Divine into oneself if The Divine already resides within us? Actually, this is best explained in terms of a magnetic field because it is an unseen tremendous force that can do equally tremendous work. A prayer (or an invocation), then acts as an inductive force to connect humankind and The Divine together. Naturally, the stronger your magnetic field, the stronger it will reach out, therefore the stronger your honest and sincere petition to reach The Divine, the more likely spiritual connection, answered prayers, realization of goals, and inner peace and harmony will be realized.

Evoke could just as easily be used in a ceremony instead of the word invoke. The terms invoke and evoke have become interchangeable over the years. The meaning of the term *evocation* is to bring the Divine into the circle but not into the body of the practitioner. Evocation is the concept and/or act of asking the angels or the Divine to be present in the circle. If you choose to be a stickler for details in your ritual, then evoke is the term to use if you do not wish the elements or the Trinity to manifest in the practitioner or the ritual tools. Instead, the Trinity comes near to the Circle for Divine protection, guidance, and cosmic balance.

Statement of Purpose/Ritual Observance

This is the appropriate place for the statement of purpose of the ceremony within the worship circle. Speak the purpose proudly and aloud to the whole circle, stating the reason of the worship gathering, whether it is an Esbat, Kyriat, or a Sabbat. Truly, the coning of power begins at this point of declaration of purpose and it continues to build through the entire ceremony until it hits its apex during the chanting or coning of power. This power is then released toward the goal the Worship Circle.

Many additional rituals can be constructed and observed throughout the year, there is no need to wait for a traditional Esbat, Kyriat, or Sabbat. For example, a Valentine's Day Ceremony can be used to celebrate love: the love The Divine has for humankind, the love that Trinitarians have for the Trinity, the love a couple has for each other, and the meditations of love we all have for family and friends.

Many worship circles come together on behalf of others or the special request of members of the Circle. It is common for the Circle to assemble in the event of an illness in the community or within an individual's family. The focus of this observance is good health, prayers of blessings toward recovery, and petitions to the Divine for assistance in healing.

It is not greedy or selfish to gather a worship circle for the petition of financial prosperity and financial assistance. Many times unforeseen bills, injury or illness can cause a seemingly endless streak of monetary opposition; this is merely an unpleasant fact. As children of The Divine, we should establish a relationship with the Holy Trinity, so that we can seek celestial help; no one should feel awkward about this type of petition for help.

Fortification of power towards a positive goal that does not invade another's personal will or freedom of choice is very acceptable. Most Wiccans of all traditions personally agree that protection spells on behalf of another is not a spiritual working that requires the permission of the recipient of the intended blessings; this is just like keeping others in your prayers.

It is just as important to gather to give thanks to The Divine. In order for proper cosmic and spiritual balance and flow between humankind and The Divine, there must be a two-way street: giving and receiving of prayers and thankfulness. Therefore, some circle observances are for general praise and worship, communing with your fellow Christian Wiccans in union with The Divine.

While these gatherings are serious, there is no need for dogmatic somberness; many fundamental Christians tend to believe church services should be serious and there is no room for celebration until they reach heaven. On the other hand, traditional Wiccans believe in making each day a holiday and celebrating their union with The Divine. Try to understand the true meaning of Living Wicca for Jesus; after all, the Holy Bible does tell us to rejoice in the Lord!

The Actual Ceremony of the Observance

All ceremonies follow the same structure starting and ending the same. What differentiates one day of power from the others is the time of year and the meaning of the ceremony, as well as the intent of the ritual. Wiccan Sabbats are very much like modern holidays, but include spiritual overtones. Actually, the bases for the majority of Christian holidays are on the seasonal observations of the earth-based religions. The Wheel of the Year contains eight sabbats. The four major sabbats are Samhain, Imbolg, Beltane, and Lughnasadh. The four lesser sabbats are observed on the equinoxes: Yule (Winter Solstice), Ostara (Spring Equinox), Litha or Mid-Summer (Summer Solstice), and Mabon (Fall Equinox).

Esbats are observances of the female aspect of the Divine, and are associated with the 4 phases of the moon. The Goddess appears in a feminine Trinity form of the Maiden, the Mother, and the Crone. These titles represent the three stages of every woman's life. Lunar rites correspond closely with women as the Waxing Moon represents the Maiden, an unwed youthful girl. The crescent moon directed toward the left symbolizes the New Moon. The rituals surrounding the Maiden aspect of the waxing moon (or gaining moon) are growth and development. Prosperity and plans for success are the key focal points of a New Moon Rite. The Full Moon represents the Mother aspect of the Goddess. This is a time for psychic work and divination. The Waning Moon represents the Crone, the diminishing crescent moon that is facing toward the right. One of the main rituals involved with the Crone is banishing.

Raising the Cone of Power

We can define cone of power in a worship Circle as the unification of personal power (one's own power within) with the other members of the circle. This personal power unites among the members of the Circle. Like in the invocation example, our personal power *arcs* to the power of The Divine, combining to make an extremely powerful, and personal spiritual experience. This is the perfect time to use this natural, personal, and Divine energy towards a positive goal. It is common for many people to feel light-headed, dizzy, or even faint if they enter into this powerful situation without being prepared for it.

Achieving the Cone the Power comes in many ways and all are equally acceptable if energy raised is the result. Vibrating, humming, chanting, and drumming are all legitimate ways to raise energy. Usually the practitioner spread their hands openly by their side with the palms open and toward the center of the circle. As the chanting or vibrating increases, the practitioners' hands and arms should naturally rise upward; eventually the circle members will feel a natural time to clasp hands. There should be no time limit nor worry for the length or the shortness of the techniques used to raise the cone of power.

A brief interview with a former Charismatic Christian turned Christian or Trinitarian Wiccan provided a wealth of knowledge in regards to the parallels between the Charismatic practicing of "receiving the Spirit" and the coning of power in a Wiccan Circle. The fact that the energies raised and experienced by the Charismatics is very similar to the personal, natural and Divine spiritual energy rush found in a Wiccan Circle, seems to follow a common thread.

She explained, "Coning the power in any tradition of Wiccan worship circle is similar to the 'Moving of the Holy Spirit' by Pentecostal or Charismatic Christian churches." When I asked her to describe what it feels like, she replied, "Well, you kind of lose yourself in the presence of The Divine, you feel that the power to work miracles is granted to you."

She continued, "The Pastor anoints a person who needs a miracle with oil and says a prayer, many times the rest of the congregation would join in, all laying hands on the person or holding their hands out in the general direction."

Looking at the components of these events summed up the logical question: "So in essence, you coned power, focused it toward a goal and released it resulting in magick?" Actually, I should have used the word 'miracle' in this question, but the answer was still "yes, pretty much." So again, we see semantics hard at work in this particular example.

The Great Rite

The celebration of The Great Rite is the miniature version of Beltane, celebrated each May 1. The Great Rite is the ceremony that celebrates the union of the God and Goddess, or the male and female principles of the Almighty One, The All: the genderless Creator and Spirit.

Many traditions of Wicca celebrate this union with variations of symbolism. Some place the phallic athame ceremoniously and reverently into the chalice as the female symbol for the womb, as the primal act of creation from which all life springs.

However, the symbolism of this ritual often makes many Wiccans regardless of tradition uncomfortable. Even though the performance of the ceremony is only symbolic, the concept of celestial mating to form all things created on this earth may be a touchy subject for some practitioners. Everyone is different. Obviously, all Wiccan practitioners are different; it is impossible to second-guess the things that make some people blush. Yet, most Wiccans comfortably view this symbolic ceremony with the reverence and respect intended.

All traditions, including Trinitarians treat this union as a sacred marriage and with ultimate respect. Trinitarian Wiccans see this as the witness and celebration of the celestial and honorary marriage of God, the Divine Bridegroom and His Divine Bride, the Goddess.

Most Christian Wiccans use the modern marriage ceremony of the three candles, which also symbolizes The Holy Trinity. Light one candle for the Divine Bride (our Goddess in her Maiden form) and light one candle for the Divine Bridegroom (our youthful God). Together the representatives of the Celestial Couple take the bride and groom's candles and light the third candle. The lighting of the third candle represents their consummation producing all of the creation, humanity, and most importantly their Son, Jesus.

It is important to point out that observing the Great Rite is not necessary at every sabbat. Many circles do observe this ceremony at each sabbat through out the year, while others only celebrate it at Beltane.

Meditation

This is time of mental calming and meditation after coning the power and the ritual observance of The Great Rite. Meditation is one of the most important techniques for any Wiccan to perfect. The key to meditation is that it relaxes the conscious mind's hold on our own psychic awareness, which is the key to the ultimate communing with The Divine.

Many fundamental Christians who follow a more dogmatic belief system have become weary of the term 'meditation' due to the New Age Movement. It is an understandable concern, as progress resulting in personal change is always a difficult human challenge. Many question its religious implications and do not understand its simple meaning. Perhaps fundamentalists could relate to the word meditation and understand its benign meaning, if they think of it as a silent prayer and/or quiet contemplation. This is a technique that all Christians have practiced for centuries, it simply now has a more modern name. No dark influences are associated with meditation.

This introspective thought time or meditation is common among all Christian faiths before receiving Communion. It is at this time that all Christians should examine their own being, prepare their minds for humility, and be thankful for The Divine sending our Lord Jesus.

Communion

For the Christian Wiccan, Communion can hold a two-fold position in the ceremony. For over two thousand years, Communion for Christians is the solemn observation of the breaking of bread and the partaking of wine which symbolizes taking the body and blood of Christ into one's own self.

Communion is also known as the Eucharist or The Lord's Supper. Wiccans celebrate a similar ritual known as Cakes and Ale, the Simple Feast, and Earthing the Power. Practitioners can partake of Communion at all Circle gatherings. Communion is appropriate anytime the Circle finds it fitting, as well as anytime any practitioner feels the sanctity to do so.

This sacrament featuring the breaking of unleavened bread (representing The Holy Son Jesus Christ' body) and fruit of the vine: wine or dark juice (representing The Blood of the Holy Son). Luke 22:19 "This Do In Remembrance of Me."

"We implore and beseech Thee, O Heavenly Father,
To send forth our Heavenly Mother and Your Power upon
This Bread and Chalice and convert them into the Body
And Blood of Our Lord and Saviour Jesus Christ. And
Jesus said unto them, I am the bread of life: he that
Cometh to me shall never hunger; and he that believeth
On me shall never thirst."

Wafer Blessing

And the Lord Jesus took bread and He
Gave thanks, and break it, and gave unto them, saying,
"Take eat, this is my body which is given for you: this
Do in remembrance of Me."

Wine Blessing

After the same manner, also he took the
Cup and when he had supped saying, "This cup is the New
Covenant in My blood: do ye as oft as ye drink it in
Remembrance of Me."

"For as oft as ye eat this bread and drink this cup,
Ye do show the Lord's death until He comes.
For whoso eateth my flesh, and drinketh my blood hath eternal life"

However, Trinitarians can combine Communion and the ritual of Cakes and Ale to honor all aspects of the Holy Trinity. Cakes and Ale is a miniature eating and drinking feast with the male and female aspects of the Divine. Feasting and communing with one's friends, family, community, and even enemies was thought to be the most ultimate forms of respect through out Europe during pre-Christian and early Christian times.

The second use of "Cakes and Ale" is returning one's body to a stable energy condition, after raising power within the worship Circle. Food itself being a product of the Earth gently lowers the levels of mental awareness attained during the ritual. This is where we get the phrase "Earthing the power."

For the Christian Wiccan, Communion can be seen not only as the somber and respectful observance of the death of Christ, but also as a sign of the communing with the Mother-Father Deity, thereby showing ultimate homage paid to the entire celestial Family.

Closing Thoughts/Benediction

The closing thoughts or benediction is the reiteration and conclusion of the circle's primary purpose, as stated at the beginning of the ceremony or ritual.

Webster's defines *benediction* as: 1. a blessing; 2. an invocation of Divine blessing, especially at the end of a religious service; 3. blessedness; 4. in affiliation with the Roman Catholic Church, a devotional service during which a consecrated Host is exposed in the monstrance and a solemn blessing is given with the Host.

Thanking the Divine & Dismissing the Quadrants

Just as focus and reverence should be observed during the invocation of the Trinity, the elements, and the angels into your sacred space, the same reverence should be given at the end of the ceremony when they are dismissed. A solitary practitioner or a coven should thank the Divine, the elements, and angels for their presence in your circle. They should then be dismissed in the reverse order as they were invited.

Some practitioners are sticklers for independent dismissal of the elements and angels in the opposite directions of invocation. Dismiss the elements by widdershins (counterclockwise) at all sabbats and kyriats. If you follow the opposite dismissal of the elements, then at Esbats or Lunar Rites, dismiss the elements by deosil (clockwise).

Others chose to invoke the elements, God and Goddess by deosil due to the superstitions revolving around casting a Circle widdershins. Therefore, obviously they would dismiss the elements always counterclockwise starting with Uriel, the Archangel, and keeper of the watchtowers of the north, and ending with Raphael, keeper of the watchtowers of the east.

One must not confuse dismissing the quadrants with dismissing the Divine. The Divine is not dismissed, but instead should be humbly thanked and graciously asked to stay with each practitioner.

Dismissing the Circle

The first thing that all need to remember about closing the worship circle, is that there should be no rush or pressure to close the circle simply because the ritual/ceremony is completed. Because the area has been cleansed and charged with personal and Divine energy, now is a good time to remain in the circle to simply sit, embellish in the energy, and meditate. Many practitioners find this a good time for scriptural reading, divination including the runes, tarot cards, and scrying. It is also a good time for the cleansing and charging of stones and crystals.

This is the perfect time for spiritual and inner faith counseling with the other members of your particular Circle of worship. Worshipping the Christian Trinity in the manner of Wicca is no doubt going to cause many people alot of inter-family stress, as well as pressure and questions from friends and onlookers. After the ceremony and before the closing of the Circle is a good time for all Christian Wiccans to try to help the ones who are receiving less than positive support from their family and friends.

Suggested Circle Closing statements:

We thank the angels - May they go in glory
We thank the elements - May they go in power
We thank The Divine that They may never leave us
For Thine is the Kingdom!
I call this Circle Open but Never Broken!
Blessed Be!
[Blessed Be!]

Merry We Meet and Merry We Part,
And Merry We Meet Again!
Blessed Be!
[Blessed Be!]

Ceremonies and Rituals

The ceremonies and rituals laid out in this section are intended to be written in an all-purpose format. They are less intricate than most group rituals you will find pre-written which assign parts to specific elder, priest(s), priestess(es) and coveners, because each Worship Circle should choose their own way of arranging their ceremonies.

On the other hand, the ceremonies and rituals are lengthier than the average pre-written rituals for solitaires, but as a result, s/he may enjoy a longer and more involved ceremony or cut it down as each practitioner sees fit.

Circles following the Christian tradition of Wicca may be rare for a while, so until a solitaire finds a group for worship, there is no reason they should not have an equally full-filling Esbat, Sabbat or Kyriat.

Esbats

Celebrating the Christian Goddess:
The Female Principle of the Divine

Wiccans of all Traditions hold lunar celebrations of the Goddess according to the phases of the moon. The most important of course, is the full moon; we call these holidays *Esbats*. They are regular meetings held by the members of the Circle, at which time the female principle of the Divine is recognized. The word "esbat" comes from the French word *esbattre*, which means, "to frolic." The moon itself is not the embodiment of the Goddess nor celebrated or worshiped as such, however, She is symbolized by the Moon. Even in the Book of Psalms in the Bible, the moon is referred to by the feminine pronoun *she*, as the sun is referred to by the masculine pronoun *he*.

Esbats primarily take place during the New and Full Moons. They can be held at any time of the month, but Wiccans consider the Full Moon Esbat, to be the most important.

This 28-day cycle is very important to female practitioners, as it is a balancing technique of the female spiritual body with the physical body. The moon is on the same monthly cycle as the female body for reproductive aspects, as well as overall feminine health and well-being.

The main additions to Esbats include the ritual of *Drawing Down the Moon*, in which the practitioners literally take the lunar powers of the Goddess into themselves. *The Charge of the Goddess* is usually recited at this time. The Charge was written by Doreen Valiente as an affirmation that the Goddess is always with us, even though She maybe forgotten by most of society.

The Full Moon occurs 13 times a year. These meetings can take place indoor or outdoors, or even in the member's home when the weather is not suitable for comfortable worship.

Full Moon Names

January - Wolf Moon. This full moon is named for the ritual observance of protection. The Wolf protects and guards its home, family, and territory. Good fortunes, change of luck and household protection are all associated ceremonies with the Wolf Moon.

February - Storm Moon. This full moon is named for the acknowledging of the end of the long nights, cold weather, and the season of death. This ritual is good for planning for the spring, family peace, blessing the boundaries of your home and celebrating Valentine's Day.

March - Chaste Moon. This full moon is named for the recognition of spring. We consider all things in nature to be virginal, fresh, and blooming at this time. It is a time for new beginnings and rituals should reflect this by warding off negative energies and poverty, while making plans for the warm months ahead.

April - Growing Moon. This full moon reflects the sowing of seeds and a new time of growth. Rituals should include the planting of seasonal crops and acknowledging the new cycle of life. This is the time for putting winter plans into action.

May - Hare Moon. This full moon is associated with the rabbit because of its symbolic procreation of life itself. The ceremonies may include the aspects of spring-cleaning, life renewal, and purification, as well as Memorial Day activities.

June - Dyad Moon. This full moon is named from the Latin word Dyad meaning two; indicating a pair or a set of twins. It is at this point that the days and nights are equal in length and the male and female forces of nature are in balance. Rituals should reflect an equal love for the male and female principles of the Divine.

July - Meade Moon. This full moon recognizes the Festival of Ale in Old Europe, a time for making wines and ales, which were made from Meade. Ale was instrumental in the simple feast of "Cakes and Ale" akin to Christian Communion. Ceremonies should include thanks for religious freedom and making plans for new goals.

August - Harvest Moon. This full moon indicates the first of the three traditional harvests. This marks the time for the beginning of canning and preserving. Rituals are bread oriented, with a strong emphasis on the harvesting of crops, gardens, or the good fortune of the work you have accomplished in previous months.

September - Barley Moon. This full moon is associated with the second and largest harvest of the year. This esbat is a time for elaborate fall celebration including the autumn equinox. Ceremonies are thanksgiving-oriented.

October - Blood Moon. This full moon is affiliated with blood due to the beginning of hunting seasons and animal slaughters to prepare food for the winter. This month is the third and final harvest. October 31 ends the Wiccan calendar and rituals this month should deal with banishing bad habits and purification of one's life and house.

November - Snow Moon. This full moon is named for the association of the coming of winter, symbolized by snow. The start of the season of death to the wheel of the year is a good time for reflection. Rituals should focus on the positive aspects of our lives and making plans to dispose of dead weight in our physical, spiritual, and emotional lives.

December - Oak Moon. This full moon is named after the mighty oak tree, which stands strong through the months of winter. The oak is a sign of strength to practitioners during the dreary winter months. Ceremonies of success and prosperity are often associated with the colors of green and brown, the colors of the leaves, and the color.

Random 13th Moon - Blue Moon. This is when a full moon that happens twice within a calendar month. This moon is a variable as to when it will happen, thus giving rise to the old saying "once in a blue moon". A blue moon is considered very lucky and all magickal workings during lunar ceremonies are extremely positive; this is a perfect time for prosperity and good luck workings.

Materials Needed for Esbats:

The Altar should be in the center of the Circle of worship. The altar cloths can be any color. However, ritual color schemes can embellish the ceremony. For example, a black and white altar cloth could symbolize the night sky and the white moon. It can also represent the Black Pillar of the Tree of Life as designated as the feminine pillar and white as the color used for the symbolism of purity.

The Three Trinity candles used during the Great Rite are typical white. However, Esbats do not usually observe the Great Rite. Instead, the Trinity

Candles used are red for Jesus, white for the Father and black for the Mother in a special candle lighting ceremony that represents all three aspects of the Christian Godhead. Place this ritual after the Invocation and before Drawing Down the Moon.

As much silver as possible should be worn by the practitioners on the night of any Esbat. Silver is a tremendous psychic conductor and is the metal associated with the moon. To reinforce this natural tool for empowerment, silver candle sticks, the silver chalice and Communion tray, and the silver bowls for blessed water, should all be found on the altar. Silver colored items and white glasswork help to create a beautiful altar.

Other symbols associated with the moon are white flowers, salt, and the gem called moonstone. A nice decorative addition to the Circle of Worship is any seasonal blooming white flower; decorating the altar, itself with these flowers adds to the visual beauty. Adorn the Circle with plenty of white candles (even marking the parameter of the Circle).

Other herbs and flowers often used in Lunar Rites are all night-blooming flowers or white flowers. These flowers include jasmine, carnations, gardenia, the lily, iris, and white roses.

The concept of white roses is a southern tradition for Mother's Day, in which we present our earthly mothers with white roses if her mother has left this earthly realm. This is a maternal sign of respect. Using this ideology, one can adorn the circle with white roses, white rose buds, and the altar with white rose petals as a tribute to our Celestial Mother, who is of another realm.

The perimeter of the Worship area can also be marked with salt. The Gospel of Philip makes notice that the Goddess Sophia is often referenced as "the salt" and the disciples did not know how to properly have their meal without salt. Salt purifies and consecrates the worship area; salt is also white and fits the over all scheme of this night of Glory to The Lady Divine.

The Casting of the Circle is very important. It should be 9 feet in diameter, as nine is the number of the Goddess, and the numerical value assigned to the moon. However, when working indoors the circle size will have to vary, so this detail should not be a point of concern as it is the overall intent of the practitioners, not the letter-perfect execution of the service.

Pre-Ceremony Preparation

Purification of Self: a purification bath with Roses (white if available)
Attunement Tea: Red Raspberry Leaf Tea
Anointing Oil: Moon Oil
Incense: Sandalwood

Semi-Precious Stones: Moonstone and Amethyst

Assemble your worship altar

The Altar should be in the center of the Circle.
The Altar cloths should be black and white.
The Chalice for the Fruit of the Vine (wine or grape juice) and
The tray of Bread for Communion is needed.

Consecrate the Intended Sacred Area by the Elements

Four conveners should walk the parameters of the circle once proclaiming the purification by the four elements using four elements separately: holy water, incense, non-iodine salt, and a candle. Remember, we affiliate the elements of Earth and Water with the Mother God and we affiliate the elements of Air and Fire with the Father God. Therefore, it may be more appropriate in a mixed Circle, for the female practitioners to perform the Earth and Water consecration responsibilities and a male practitioner to perform the Fire and Air consecration responsibilities.

The first covener should ask the Goddess to consecrate the Water towards the goal of purifying the Circle in the name of the Lady Divine and then sprinkle the water just inside the parameters. Likewise, the second covener should ask the Goddess to consecrate the salt which represents the element of Earth toward the goal of purifying the Circle in the name of the Lady Divine and sprinkle the salt within the edges of parameter of the Circle.

The third covener should then ask the God or male aspect of the Divine to consecration the Fire towards the goal of purifying the Circle in the name of the Lord Divine and walk the parameters of the Circle with the lit candle. Then lastly, the fourth covener should petition the Lord Divine with the incense, representing the element of Air toward the goal of purifying the Circle. The fourth covener should walk the parameters of the Circle waving the incense in symbolic spirals or in the pattern of the pentacle at each quadrant point.

Combining the elements of Earth (salt) and
Water (requesting the blessings of
The Mother Goddess) to sprinkle the Sacred Area
Followed by Fire and Air in the form of incense
(Requesting the blessings of The Father God).

Casting a Christian Circle of Worship

On Esbats, cast the Circle by widdershins or walking counterclockwise, using your projective hand to direct the energy within you into a circle around you. Some practitioners use an athame; others may use only their hand.

Remember to always keep your receiving hand (your left hand usually if you are right handed) palm down for grounding. You can move your entire body around the parameters of the circle or only your projecting hand while standing at the center of the circle. Regardless of your technique, due to the intent of perfect love and perfect trust, the desired results will be the same.

Casting the Circle

[Walk the Perimeter of the Circle Twice]
I conjure Thee O Sacred Circle of Power
In the Name of the Holy Mother, Father and Son!
I call upon your Presence and Blessings
Of this Lunar Rite
As the Three Shall Be One!

[Walk the Circle a Third Time and Say]
I Declare this Circle Properly Cast and Protected
by The Holy Trinity!

Assembling the Quadrants

[Invoke/Invite the angels, archangels, spirits and/or
keepers of the Watchtowers, the directions,
the elements, and Powers that reside in them.]

Hail to the Ladies of the Watchtowers Of the East
Keepers of the Powers of Wind and Air
We invoke thee!
Be With Us and Bless Us
This Night of Lunar Worship

Hail to the Ladies of the Watchtowers Of the South
Keepers of the Powers of Fire and Flame
We invoke thee!

Be With Us and Bless Us
This Night of Lunar Worship

Hail to the Ladies of the Watchtowers Of the West
Keepers of the Powers of Water and Intuition
We invoke thee!
Be With Us and Bless Us
This Night of Lunar Worship

Hail to the Ladies of the Watchtowers Of the North
Keepers of the Powers of Mother Earth
We invoke thee!
Be With Us and Bless Us
This Night of Lunar Worship

The Invocation of the Goddess

Hail to Our Goddess!
The Most Glorious Mother Spirit
Our Luminous Lady Divine:
Holy is Your Place in Heaven!
We ask you to be One with Us
Celebrating this Full Moon Rite
We feel your lunar energies come nigh
Our Celestial Mother rules the Night Sky.

We Invoke Thee - Great Goddess!!
The Mother of All Living Things
The Mother of Our Loving Saviour:
She Who Is Hope and Angel's Wings.
Come now and Descend upon us:
Bathe us in Our Lady's love,
In our Perfect Circle - forever floating on the pure
White wings of a dove!
Holy Mother, Spirit of Righteousness
Bless Us this Night, Dear Goddess!

Statement of Purpose

Hail Sisters and Brothers!
We Gather Tonight on this (Month's) Eve
For the Monthly Full Moon
As We Celebrate this Lunar Rite and
To honour the female principle
Of the Divine God Pair:
She is our Goddess

She is Our Mighty Heavenly Mother!
We gather to glorify and Commune
With The Supernal Goddess and
Queen of Heaven!

While so many of Christ's Children have
Forgotten You Holy Mother
Tonight, We Assemble to
Show that we have Not!

Lend us your Wisdom and Understanding
Show us Your Divine Love
O Dear Celestial Goddess,
The Divine Bride of our God
Be With Us Tonight in our Worship!

The Candle Light Ceremony

[The Priest and Priestess or Elder should position himself or herself in a benevolent pose and begin to light the three candles]

(The Elder lights the black candle for the Female principle of The Divine)

We Invoke Thee,
O Blessed Goddess
Who Dwells Among Us!
She, Who is Understanding
Commune with Us Tonight
As we celebrate you, Our Lady Divine.

(The Elder lights the white candle for the male principle of The Divine)
We Invoke Thee,
Father in Heaven
Come Be Among Us!
He, Who is Wisdom,
Watch Over Us Tonight
As we celebrate Our Lady Divine.

(The Elder lights the red candle for the Child principle of The Divine)
We Invoke Thee,
The Only Begotten Son
Come Be Among Us!
He, Who is Mercy and Compassion,
Bless Us Tonight
As we celebrate Our Lady Divine.

Charge of the Goddess

Listen now my children to the words of the Great Mother,
Creatrix of the Universe, She who Is
The Spirit that Moved Upon the Waters
In times of old, I am called by many names among
All of Humanity:
Asherah, Sophia, Mother Mary, the Holy Spirit,
Mary Magdalene, Eloi, the Bride, Levannah, and Jerah.
I am that I am. I am your Goddess.
I am the Mother of all Living Things,
I am the Mother of my only Begotten Son,
In Whom, I am well pleased.

Whenever ye have need of any thing, once in the month,
Better it be when the moon is full,
Assemble yourself in some secret place,
And adore the Spirit of the Divine,
Who is Queen of Heaven.

I am the gracious Goddess,
Who gives the gift of joy unto the heart of the world.
Upon earth, I give the knowledge of the spirit eternal; and
Beyond death, I give peace, freedom, and reunion

With those who have gone before.
I do not demand sacrifice; for behold,
I am the Mother of all living,
And my love is poured out upon the earth

I am the beauty of the Green Mother Earth,
The White Moon among the stars,
And the mystery of the waters:
The Upper and the Lower Firmament.
I am the warmth in the hearts of all humanity.

Call upon your soul; arise and come unto Me;
For I am the Soul of the World, She who gives Life to the Universe.
From Me all things proceed, and Unto Me
All things must return;
And before my face, beloved of God and of men,
Let Thine innermost Divine self be enfolded
In the rapture of the infinite.

Let My worship make melody in your hearts;
For behold, all acts of Love and Kindness are my rituals.
Therefore let there be beauty and strength,
Power and compassion, honour and humility,
Mirth and reverence within you.

And thou who thinkest to seek for me, know thy seeking
Yearning shall avail thee not unless thou knowest the mystery:
That if that which thou Seekest thou Findest not within,
Thou wilt never find it without.
For behold, I have been with you from the beginning;
And I am that which is attained at the end of desire.

Drawing Down the Moon

We Prepare Now to Draw Down the Spirit of the Moon!
Our Luminous Goddess,
We summon Thee and Invoke Thee
Mighty Mother of us all.
Symbol of Delicate Beauty and Understanding
With Your Unsurpassed Strength
Be With us tonight!!

As we Raise Our Hands
We Feel the Energy of your Divine Love
In our Fingertips - In our Hearts
And In our Soul.
We hold our Hands Upwards toward the heavens
To feel your Motherly Touch
We stand together in Praise
We invoke Thee to Descend upon this Circle
And Pour out your Light and Loving Grace
Tonight - Fulfill Us
As We Draw Down the Moon

Prayer of the Lady Divine

O Hail to the fair moon,
Our orb of the night;
Symbolizing our Mother in Heaven
Until the morning light
Beloved Mother by the full moon
Shine Down With Delight
And Guide our Minds and Hearts
Like the Oceans and Tides

The Moon, She is appointed for seasons:
For when the Sun is going down.
The Sun shall not smite thee by day, nor the Moon by night.
Shall we be established forever as the Moon,
And as a faithful witness in Heaven?

Blow Up the Trumpet in the New Moon,
In the Time Appointed
On Our Solemn Feast Day.
The Sun to rule by day,
The Moon and Stars to rule by night.

Behold O Sun of Righteousness
The Moon Is Full and Our Mother
The Triple Goddess is One Tonight:
Maiden, Mother, and Crone
Earth and Heaven are One

And we are One with The All

Blessed Be Our Mother Spirit
[Blessed Be!]
Blessed Be Our Lady Divine
[Blessed Be!]
Blessed Be the Mother of our Saviour Jesus Christ
[Blessed Be!]

Procession of Names

[The members should walk the Circle widdershins. The many names of the Mother are called one by one and honored by the entire Circle. This can be executed as statements by the Priest, Priestess, Elder, or leader of the Circle; the procession of names can also be executed as call and reply with the members of the Circle.]

Heavenly Mother - Fair Goddess:
You are Known by many Names
Among your Christian Children.
We call for you:
The Shekinah, Asherah,
Inanna, Sophia,
The Holy Spirit, Elohim, the Virgin Mary,
Mary Magdalene.

Hail to the Shekinah!
[Blessed Be the Goddess!]
Hail Asherah!
[Blessed Be the Goddess!]
Hail Inanna!
[Blessed Be the Goddess!]
Hail Sophia!
[Blessed Be the Goddess!]
Hail to the Holy Spirit!
[Blessed Be the Goddess!]
Hail Elohim!
[Blessed Be the Goddess!]
Hail to the Virgin Mary!
[Blessed Be the Goddess!]
Hail Mary Magdalene!
[Blessed Be the Goddess!]

[Hailed by the leader of the Circle:]

Through these words we have uttered
Through these names we have called
The Presence of the Lady Divine
Dwells among Us!
Let us Adore Her
Let us Be Thankful
Let us Praise Her
She is Her Holiness!!

Blessed Be the Trinity

Blessed Be unto the Holy Trinity:
Blessed Be the Mother, the Father,
And the Holy Son!
[Blessed Be the Trinity!]

Blessed Be the Goddess, On this Lunar Rite
Shine on us Mother - thy Heavenly Light!
[Blessed Be the Mother!]

Blessed Be Our God, the Infinite One
Father of Jesus Christ, the Symbol of the Sun!
[Blessed Be the Father!]
Blessed Be to Our Lord, Who Died on the Cross
Our Saviour and King, So that None maybe Lost!
[Blessed Be the Son!]

We Give Thanks for All the Blessings We Receive
We Give Thanks and We Give Praise
Blessed Be to the Holy Trinity
As we feel the Divine Powers Raise!

Blessed be the Divine
[Blessed Be!]
Blessed be The One
[Blessed Be!]
Blessed be the Triune God
[Blessed Be!]
Blessed be the Spirit of Old - Blessed be the Spirit of The All
[Blessed Be! - Blessed Be!]

Let Us Now Thank the Holy Trinity
For All of the Blessings that We Receive
We Give Thanks and We Give Praise
Blessed Be to the Holy Trinity
As we feel the Divine Powers Raise!

Circle chant - Raising the Cone of Power

Lady Divine - Spirit Moonlight - Goddess Above - Bless Us Tonight
Lady Divine - Spirit Moonlight - Goddess Above - Bless Us Tonight
Lady Divine - Spirit Moonlight - Goddess Above - Bless Us Tonight
[Continue the Chant as long as Needed]

Releasing the Cone of Power

Let Us Now Release this Divine Energy
Into the World to Comfort and Protect
All that is lacking in the presence of the Mother Spirit
As She is, true Nurturing and true Understanding:
May She Bless All in Her Divine Path!
Blessed Be!
[Blessed Be!]

Time for Meditation and Reflection

Communion

Circle Fellowship

[Passing of the white candle]
I rejoice with my Circle gathered tonight
To praise The Lady Divine as I
Pass this white light:
(Personal desire or petition spoken here)

Parting Prayer & Songs

Closing Thoughts/Benediction

This Lunar Rite is now Ended
Our Beloved Goddess has been Honored
And we have felt her Loving Touch Tonight
Divine Mother we ask you to dwell within us always!
Guard Us and Guide Us
In Perfect Love and Perfect Trust.
Bless us with your Knowledge and Vision to See
If It Be your Will - So Mote it Be!
[So Mote It Be!]

Thanking the Deities

As we humbly thank all the elements, spirits,
Fairies and the Angels for being with us this Lunar Rite
To Honour our Goddess, Queen of Heaven!
We acknowledge our the Holy Trinity:
Jesus and the Lord and Lady Divine,
We ask you to stay if you will or go if you must
As we are always comforted
In Perfect Love and Perfect Trust!
Blessed Be!
[Blessed Be!]

Dismissing the Quadrants

We wish to thank the Ladies of the Watchtowers
Of the North, who command Mother Earth
For being with us
This Night of Lunar Worship
Stay If you Will - Go if you Must
Hail and Farewell!
[Hail and Farewell!]

We wish to thank the Ladies of the Watchtowers
Of the West, who command the Waters, Oceans, and Lakes
For being with us
This Night of Lunar Worship
Stay if you Will - Go if you Must
Hail and Farewell!

[Hail and Farewell!]

We wish to thank the Ladies of the Watchtowers
Of the South, who command Fire and Flame
For being with us
This Night of Lunar Worship
Stay if you Will - Go if you Must
Hail and Farewell!
[Hail and Farewell!!]

We wish to thank the Ladies of the Watchtowers
Of the East, who command The Air and Blowing Winds
For being with us
This Night of Lunar Worship
Stay if you Will - Go if you Must
Hail and Farewell
[Hail and Farewell!]

Dismissing the Circle

Kyriats and Sabbats

Sabbats and Esbats are the days and nights of power; these are normal celebrations or rituals observed by Traditional Wiccans, who view The Young Solar God from the perspective that He grows up to become the Father God. This is essentially viewing the Mother Goddess and the Father God aspect of the One Spirit recognized and represented by the Wheel of the Year, or the annual cycles of nature. Since the One Spirit is regarded as "Deus et Natura" (Latin for "God and Nature") to our planet, Traditional Wiccans believe there is no better way to honour the Father-God, the Mother God, and the Young Sun God than through the spiritual biorhythms of the seasons.

All Christians should be able to equate this view of the Trinity as Jehovah (the Father), The Mother (the Holy Spirit), and the Son (Sun) as the Solar God or the Young Male God. In Traditional Wiccan Circles, the Infant God is born at Christmas (or Yule) and grows through the year as nature blooms and flurishes and becomes the Father God who is aged and dies at Halloween (or Samhain), as all natures prepares for Winter sleep and hibernation before the cycle repeats.

However, in Christianity, the three aspects of the Divine Trinity do not waver in age and status. Regardless of Jesus' earthly age, Christians celebrate His birth, the teachings and ministries, as well as the death and resurrection at non-linear times of the year.

Many earth-based religions view the Trinity aspects inside both the God and the Goddess. In the female principle of the Godhead, we commonly hear of the Maiden, the Mother, and the Crone. This is the young goddess, the mother aspect of the Goddess, and the wise woman who is past child-birthing years but is a fortress of practical knowledge and wisdom. It is a little known fact that in earth-based religions, there is a Male Trinity regarded as the Son, the Husband/Father, and the Sage.

Because Christ and His teaching is the focal point of the Christian religion and spiritual path, a sabbat for Jesus separate of the Mother (Esbats) and the Father (Sabbats) should be observed. I coined the term "kyriat" from the Greek phrase "Kyrie Eleeson" which means "Lord [Jesus Christ] have mercy." This Greek phrase is used in Psalm 123:3 as "Have mercy upon us, O Lord, have mercy upon us: for we are exceedingly filled with contempt".

Therefore, on the cardinal points of the year, the equinoxes, and solstices, Christian Wiccans can celebrate Kyriats, which are Jesus-oriented Sabbat rituals. Kyriats can be defined as "holidays that celebrate the Wheel of the Year as it applies to the life of Jesus."

1. Ostara, Spring Equinox, or the Vernal Equinox is the traditional name for this lesser sabbat. This is a good time to recognize the beginning and the end of Christ's days on this earth (Trinitarian Wiccans observe the Alpha and the Omega Kyriat). This is because many historians believe the time of the birth of Jesus was approximately three weeks within the timeframe of his crucifixion; therefore, this day of observance falls into the Wiccan cycle of his birth-death- and rebirth into heaven. For traditional Wiccans, this is a solar festival, in which day and night, and the forces of male and female, are equally balanced.

2. Litha, Midsummer, or Summer Solstice is for tradition Wiccans. For the Trinitarian Wiccans, it is the Baptismal Kyriat which celebrates the prophecies of the birth of Jesus and his cousin John the Baptist, the preaching and baptizing of John the Baptist proclaiming the coming of Jesus, and then the actual Baptism of Jesus Christ, our Lord and Saviour. This is a perfect time for renewing one's vows of baptism with the anointing of water. Ironically aligned with the Catholic Church's observation and Christianization of this holy day, making it John the Baptist Day, the Baptismal Kyriat fits perfectly into the Wheel of Christ's Life.

3. Mabon or the Autumn Equinox celebrates the feast of the second harvest among the farming communities and earth-based religions of Europe. For Christians, we can also take part in this

feast of Thanksgiving as the Feast Kyriat when Jesus fed the
multitude.
4. Yule, Christmas, or the Winter Solstice is also the time of the
Messianic Kyriat. This is a Holy Day (holiday) dedicated to the
celebration of the pentacle of the life of Christ: His Ministry,
His Multitudes of earthly followers, and the Great Works
performed by the Living Jesus. Handal's Messiah directly
influences the name of this Kyriat, as this majestic piece of
orchestrations written and intended to proclaim Jesus Christ as
the King of Kings, Lord of Lords, and the Prince of Peace.

Yule Sabbat, the Messianic Kyriat
Christmas and Winter Solstice:
December 22

The winter solstice marks the longest night of the year. The traditional
folk meaning of Yule is that the Goddess awakens to find that she is
pregnant with the Solar God. The intent of the rituals for both the summer
and winter solstices are to help change the course of the Sun, which directly
affected the crops, the growing seasons, and the healthy rhythms of the
human body. With the aid of the Sun, the symbol of the Young Solar God,
the farmers have reassurance of a vibrant spring and the blessings of the
plentiful harvests in autumn.

The Roman Catholic Church then Christianized the Winter Solstice or
Yule as Christmas, or Christ Mass. Christmas celebrates the birth of Jesus at
Yule, regardless of the possibility that the spring or the summer months may
be more accurate. The Catholic Church held special ceremonies to take the
place of Yule for the former earth-based religions now encompassed by the
established church.

The season of winter has been the time observed for the birth of the
young Solar God in many cultures for thousands of years. Keeping the Yule
custom, the Roman Catholic Church assigned Jesus' birth to the schedule of
the birth of the Young God as in the Pagan cultures.

Yule and Christmas have always been associated with the spirit of
giving, just as The Magi, or the Magicians, came bearing gifts to the Christ
child. The Winter Holy Days of Power are symbolic of the joy of giving to
others for centuries, regardless of the culture. Customs vary all over the
world with the childhood celebrations of the Holy King, Old Saint Nick,
Mother Berhta, and Santa Claus.

The colors affiliated with Winter Solstice, Yule, and Christmas are red,
green, white, and gold. It is easy to guess the herbs and plants associated

with Yule because the tradition has carried on to our modern Christmas celebrations.

The herbs associated with Yule are holly, ivy, and mistletoe. Yule herbs used as incense associated with Yule are frankincense and myrrh. The odors of cinnamon and nutmeg are just as common today to the celebration of Christmas as thousands of years ago with the celebration of Yule, or even just a few hundred years ago in Europe before the colonization of the States.

The symbol of decorating a small potted evergreen at Yule/Christmas has been tradition since early Pagan celebrations. Other symbols include topping the Yule trees with the Triple Moon, which is the symbol of the Maiden, Mother and the Crone aspects of the Goddess. After the Christianization of Yule, the star topped the tree. This affiliation with Christ is symbolic of the Star of Bethlehem, ironically the pentacle of the five elements. Angels also became part of the Roman Catholic adaptation of Yule as symbols of the celestial messengers crowning the evergreen tree. Many ChristoWiccans feel the use of the Star atop of the tree, lends a dual purpose to this hybrid path of Jesus and the Mother.

Colonial and Early American Christmas used the decorations of Mother Nature. Apples, oranges, lemons, and pineapples adorn doors and boughs, just as they did in the pre-Christian Europe. Holly, mistletoe, pinecones, and evergreens are wonderful seasonal decorations not only for the home, but also for the altar. This is the season for the burning of the Yule Log.

Old Religion Deities: The Spinning Goddess: Gaia (Greek), Eve (Hebrew), Shekinah (Hebraic-Gnostic), the Virgin Mary (Christian-Gnostic), and the Spinning Woman (Native American). All Reborn Sun Gods: Apollo (Greco-Roman), Janus (Roman), Lugh (Irish), the Oak/Holly King (Anglo-Celtic), Ra (Egyptian), Father Sun (Native American), Jesus (Christian-Gnostic), Odin (Norse), and Mithras (Persian).

Contents Needed for the Ritual:
The Altar should be in the center of the Circle of worship. The altar cloths should be green and red keeping with the celebratory colors of the season. The Three Trinity Candles, used in the honoring of the Great Rite, should be white especially giving a nod of meaning to the purity of the snow. Decorate your Circle of Worship with pinecones, seasonal greenery and wreaths made of pine, fir, spruce, or cedar. Some Circles may wish to decorate a Yule tree to accompany their altar, if space permits, if not just at the perimeter of the sacred space. Adorn the Circle with plenty of red and green candles and Poinsettias. If a cauldron is used during the Yule celebration, it is customary to adorn it with a wreath.

This is a perfect time for Circles to draw names and exchange gifts, as well as invite your children and spouse (if they not a practicing member of the Circle) for the raising of the tree, refreshments, and seasonal rejoicing!

Pre-Ceremony Preparation

1. Purification of Self: a purification bath with Blessed Thistle.
2. Attunement Tea: Cinnamon or Apple Cinnamon
3. Oils for Anointing: Myrrh
4. Incense: Bayberry
5. Semi-Precious Stones: Garnet, Bloodstone, and Ruby

Consecrate the Intended Circle

Casting the Circle

[Walk the Perimeter of the Circle Twice]
I summons Thee O Circle of Divine Power
That you may wrap yourself around us times three
For health, Wealth and Prosperity
May the Holy Trinity protect us as we raise power and worship
This joyous night as We celebrate Yule
So, As We will it - So Mote it Be!!

[Walk the Circle a Third Time and Say]
I call this Sacred Space Cast in Perfect Christian Love and Trust!

Assembling the Quadrants

O Kind and Good Spirits of the East
Lords and Ladies of the Watchtowers
Keepers of Wind and Air
As We Follow the Sacred Star of Bethlehem
We Invoke thee!
Bless Us as we Celebrate Yule:
Jesus Christ is Born!

O Kind and Good Spirits of the South
Lords and Ladies of the Watchtowers
Keepers of Fire and Flame

As We Follow the Sacred Star of Bethlehem
We Invoke thee!
Bless Us as we Celebrate Yule:
Jesus Christ is Born!

O Kind and Good Spirits of the West
Lords and Ladies of the Watchtowers
Keepers of Water and Intuition
As We Follow the Sacred Star of Bethlehem
We Invoke thee!
Bless Us as we Celebrate Yule:
Jesus Christ is Born!

O Kind and Good Spirits of the North
Lords and Ladies of the Watchtowers
As We Follow the Sacred Star of Bethlehem
Keepers of Mother Earth
We Invoke thee!
Bless us as we Celebrate Yule:
Jesus Christ is Born!!

The Invocation of the GodPair

Hail to Our Lord and Lady Divine
Who Are In Heaven, Blessed be thy Names!!
Please join us in our Celebration
We Ask your blessings, understanding, and
Your Presence to be Among Us Tonight
As we Celebrate the Winter Solstice
Kind God we Invoke thee!
[Hail to Our God!]
Loving Goddess We Invoke Thee!
[Hail to Our Goddess!]
Blessed Be the GodPair
[Blessed Be!]

Statement of Purpose

Hail Brothers and Sisters!
We Gather Tonight on this December's Eve
To celebrate the winter Festival of Yule

It is the birth of The Divine Son
Our Saviour, Jesus Christ.
For Christ is the Sun of Righteousness
And in this Long Cold Winter,
The Birth of Christ promises the return of the Sun
It gives us hope and courage
As we make plans
Of renewal in the warm Months Ahead.

We stand together united in the Spirit of the Season,
When hearts are light and the love
Of Our Goddess and Our God.
Let us be Thankful for all we have:
Let us remember the Spirit of Giving
Unselfishly of Ourselves
When so many around us are in need!
Let the Solar Light Shine in Our Hearts
And in Our Minds
As the Celebration of Yule Begins!

The Winter Solstice

The Season of Winter is upon us!
The Wheel of the Year Turns onward!
Winter is the time of the Year
In which all Nature Rests.
Many of Her Animals Slumber while many Continue
To scurry about providing for their nests.

The Trees are Barren of Leaves and
Snow Lays On the Ground
The Air is Crisp and Clean.
A Winter Wonderland is truly delightful
As The Earth's Beauty Takes on a New Face.

Lighting of the Seasonal Candles

[Lighting of the White Candle]
Blessed Be the Season of Yule
Blessed Be the Virgin Mary
Earthly Mother of Our Lord Jesus Christ

For on this Night, we Celebrate!

Hear us on the Eve of this Winter's Solstice
As we assemble in the Cold and Quiet,
As we give thanks for this Winterland of enchantment
On this Longest Night of the Year!

Our Goddess Mother - Our Father God
We Thank You For
For the Many Blessings of Yule and all
The this Season stands for:
Let us Celebrate and Sing Praises!
Joy to the Heaven's on High!
We sing and dance a carol
And a-wassailing we go
The Yule log burns bright,
On this Winter's Night with smiles all a-glow
We sing and dance a carol
With the Hope of Winter's Snow.

[Lighting of the Green Candle]
Season's Blessings we now ask for Yule
This Winter Eve of Solstice Time.
We Sing and Dance and Make Merry
As we celebrate this Christmas Time.
Apples, Oranges, and Lemons:
Nature now Decorate our doors and our Boughs
Our trees brightly lit to show
Our rejoicing and our vows.

The Fresh Evergreens bring us Harmony
December Magick and the Mistletoe
The Holly and the Ivy
Sets all our hearts a-glow.
The Greenery is a promise that Spring
Will Soon be Here -
So let us make joy and melody tonight
And in our Hearts Through Out the Year!

[The Lighting of the Red Candle]
And there were in the same country
Shepherds abiding in the field

Keeping watch over their flock by Night.

And, lo, the angel of the Lord
Came upon them,
And the Glory of the Lord
Shone round about them:
And they were sore afraid.

And the angel said unto them:
Fear not: for behold, I bring you
Good Tidings of Joy,
Which shall be to all People.

For Unto Us is born this day
In the City of David
A Saviour, which is Christ the Lord
And this should be a sign unto you:
Ye shall find the babe wrapped
In swaddling clothes, lying the manger.

And Suddenly there was with the angel
A multitude of the Heavenly Hosts
Praising God, and saying,
Glory to God in the Highest,
And on Earth peace,
Good Will Toward Men.

The Messianic Kyriat

For Unto us a Child is born - Unto us a Son is given
And the Government shall be upon His Shoulders
And His name shall be called:
Wonderful, Counselor
Eternal God, the Everlasting Father
The Prince of Peace
And He shall reign forever and ever:
King of Kings and Lord of Lords

Blessed Be the Trinity

Blessed Be the Holy Trinity:
Blessed Be the Mother, the Father,
And the Holy Son!
[Blessed Be the Trinity!]

Blessed Be Our Lord, Who is born on this Day
Our Saviour and King, Forever to Reign!
[Blessed Be the Son!]

Blessed Be Goddess, the Symbols Moon and Earth
Mother of Jesus Christ, the Virginal Birth!
[Blessed Be the Mother!]

Blessed Be Our God, the Infinite One
Father of Jesus Christ, the Symbol of the Sun!
[Blessed Be the Father!]

We Give Thanks for All the Blessings We Receive
We Give Thanks and We Give Praise
Blessed Be the Holy Trinity
As we feel the Divine Powers Raise!

Blessed Be Our Goddess
The Virgin Mother of All
[Kyrie Eleeson!]
Blessed Be Our God
The Father, Our Lord Divine
[Kyrie Eleeson!]
Blessed Be Jesus Christ
The Promised Holy Son
[Kyrie Eleeson!]

Lighting of the Yule Log

The Wicca Shows Us Ways by Three
We praise The Divine as The Holy Trinity
Three Wicks are lit, And Three Thoughts Have We
For Faith, Hope and Love - So Mote It Be

[Lighting the first wick]
Faith is the reason that we cannot explain
[Lighting the second wick]
Hope is the feeling and the desire, the same
[Lighting the third wick]
Love is the purpose, In Christ Jesus' name!

Brightly Does the Yule Log Burn
Never-ending does The Wheel Turn
Banish Sickness and Evil Spurn
By the Sun of Righteousness, We Live and Learn!

Circle chant - Raising the Cone of Power

Hallelujah to the Messiah - Our Saviour is Born
The Pentacle Burns Bright Around Us - He is Christ our Lord
Hallelujah to the Messiah - Our Saviour is born
The Pentacle Burns Bright Around Us - He is Christ our Lord
Hallelujah to the Messiah - Our Saviour is born
The Pentacle Burns Bright Around Us - He is Christ our Lord
He is Christ our Lord!
He is Christ our Lord!
He is Christ our Lord!

Releasing the Power

We Release this Divine Power and Energy into the World
Who does Not Know the Mother
In the Spirit of Perfect Love and Perfect Trust!
In this Season of Giving Gifts
Let Us all be thankful of The Divine's Greatest Gift to Humankind
The Gift of our Saviour
The Lord, Jesus Christ!
Blessed Be!
[Blessed Be!]

Time for Meditation and Reflection

Communion

Circle Fellowship

[The Messianic Kyriat and Yule Sabbat can be a several hour affair. Decorating the Tree, Singing songs of the Season, New and Old Exchanging Gifts, Refreshments and Celebration]

Closing Thoughts/Benediction

This Festival of Yule has come to its end:
We Celebrate the Blessings of our
Celestial Mother and Father,
Honoring the Christ child in heart, mind, and soul!
Let tonight's Spirit of the Season
Burn Brightly in our Hearts All Year
Let us Be of Good Conscience
And Be of Good Cheer!

Thanking the Deities

Gracious God and Goddess,
O Gracious Infant Divine:
We Thank you for Being with Us Tonight
And For Blessing this Ceremony of Yule!
The Presence of Your Wisdom and Understanding
Is Our Desire for Each and Every
Ritual For Which We Gather!
Blessed Be the Holy Trinity!
[Blessed Be!]

Dismissing the Quadrants

Good and Kind Spirits of the North
Who Preside over our Mother Earth
We thank you for being with
Us this Night in the Celebration of
The Holy Birth of Christ.
Stay if you will - Go if you Must

We Bid You Hail and Farewell!
[Hail and Farewell!]

Good and Kind Spirits of the West
Who Preside over Water and Intuition
We thank you for being with
Us this Night in the Celebration of
The Holy Birth of Christ.
Stay if you Will - Go if you Must
We Bid You Hail and Farewell!
[Hail and Farewell!]

Good and Kind Spirits of the South
Who Preside over Fire and Feelings
We thank you for being with
Us this Night in the Celebration of
The Holy Birth of Christ.
Stay if you Will - Go if you Must
We Bid You Hail and Farewell!
[Hail and Farewell!]

Good and Kind Spirits of the East
Who Preside over Air and Invention
We thank you for being with
Us this Night in the Celebration of
The Holy Birth of Christ.
Stay if you Will - Go if you Must
We Bid You Hail and Farewell!
[Hail and Farewell!]

Dismissing the Circle

Imbolg, Oimelc, Britannia, or Candlemas:
February 1st and/or 2nd

This celebratory ritual is a winter festival of purification and fire, often-called "the Feast of Lights," Imbolc or Imbolg (pronounced "em bowl gee"). The term Imbolg means "in the belly" referring to ewe's milk, which marks the time pregnant ewes began lactation. It also signifies the growing of life in the womb of Mother Earth, as Imbolg brings the first signs of returning life in the darkness of winter.

Bridantia is the Celtic holy celebration honoring the Goddess Brigid. She was the Irish-Celtic goddess of fire, fertility, crops, livestock, wisdom, poetry, and household arts. Now known as Sainte Brigit, the Roman Catholic Church absorbed the Celtic Goddess of Brigid. The Goddess Brigid was very popular among the Irish and while practitioners of the Old Religion took on the new All Male Christian Trinity of the Catholic Church, they refused to give up their beloved Goddess Brigid. As opposed to loosing the entire country of Ireland, the Roman Catholic Church granted the Goddess sainthood. The festivals of the Triple Goddess Brigid become celebrations in the form of a mass on St. Brigit's Day.

When the Roman Catholic Church Christianized this sabbat, it was renamed as Candlemas. Celebrated by candlelight, processionals and commemorates the Presentation of Christ in the Temple (Eastern Church) or the Purification of the Virgin Mary (Western Church). It is also traditional to light every candle in the house to honor God after dusk.

The uncomfortable aspect of Candlemas is the treatment of the mothers at the time of the birth of Christ. In the times B.C.E., the birth process for the mother (Mary included) was considered unclean and the mother was not allowed to return to the temple until she was deemed purified and cleansed by the Church authorities. This approach to humanity is quite the opposite of the Pagan respect for birth and all forms of life, considering the entire birthing process to be of the One Spirit, natural and beautiful.

Imbolg also corresponds with Ground Hog's Day, the popular litmus test for the arrival of spring, deriving from the original use of hedgehogs in Europe. Intended to predict the coming of spring, this is a weather divination ritual. It is humorously ironic that the Americans seriously observe this Pagan ritual of practical magick without giving it a second thought.

The colors affiliated with Imbolg and Candlemas: White, Yellow, and Pink. The symbols affiliated with Imbolg and Candlemas: Candles, Burrowing Animals (such as the Ground Hog), Grain Dolly, and Sun Wheels.

Old Religion Deities: All Virgin Goddesses: Athena (Greek), Selene (Greek), Vesta (Roman); All Flame Goddesses: Brigid (Irish), Februa (Roman), Lucina (Roman-Norse). All Flame Gods: Februus (Roman), Cupid/Eros (Greco-Roman), Dumuzi (Sumerian).

Contents Needed for the Ritual:
The Altar should be in the center of the Circle of worship. The altar cloths can be green and white, symbolizing the snow of winter and green as the promise of spring. The Trinity candles should be white, emphasizing the purity of this sabbat. The practitioner needs one large, tall, white candle for

the ceremony of Candlemas. Seven day candles in glass jars work very well because of their long burn time and for safety purposes. Each participant also needs a small glass votive candle; the colors can vary.

The practitioners of the Circle can decorate with whatever flowers may have bloomed so early, and the same with greenery. An abundance of white candles is tradition for this ritual, covering the altar, the layout of the Circle; it is also common for each member of the Worship Circle to also hold a white candle. Prepare a crown or wreath of straw or vine with 13 white candles and place in the center of the altar.

Pre-Ceremony Preparation

1. Purification of Self: a purification bath with Jasmine
2. Suggested Attunement Tea: Chamomile or Rosemary
3. Anointing Oil: Neroli
4. Incense: Lavender
5. Semi-Precious Stones: Amethyst and Turquoise

Consecrate the Intended Circle

Prelude to the Celebration of Imbolg

[All should remain dark - no candles lit on the altar until after the reading of the following verses: The Priest, Priestess, priest and priestess, the duet of Priests or duet of Priestesses or the Elder should approach the altar carrying a tall white, lighted candle and recite this passage preceding the opening rites.]

In the Beginning, Elohim created
The Heaven and the Earth.
And the earth was without form and void
And darkness moved upon the face of the deep!

And the Spirit of God, The Shekinah moved
Upon the face of the waters.
And the Divine said, Let there be light:
And there was Light.

As it was in the beginning and as
It shall always be:
There is Darkness and Light.
There is Light in the Darkness,

And there is Darkness in the Light!
Seek the Divine Truth in the Darkness
And you will find the Glory of Light!

The Lighting of the Imbolg Candles

[The Priest/ess or Elder positions then begins to light the quadrant candles clockwise in the east and ending in the north. Then light the white candles of the wreath. All but the three main alter candles are then lit.]

Casting the Circle

[Walk the Perimeter of the Circle Twice]
I Call Upon the Wise and Ancient Forces
Of the Divine to Guard and Guide this Circle
Aid us To Assemble the Holy Temple
And Protect this Sacred Space
In Our Time of Praise
In the Name of the Holy Trinity
May Our Energies Gather and Raise.

[Walk the Circle a Third Time and Say
I Declare this Circle Properly Cast and Protected by The Holy Trinity!

Assembling the Quadrants

O Divine Beings of Light
Ancient and Mighty Ones of the East
Keepers of Wind and Air
Lend Us Your Power and Glory
Protect Us this Night of Imbolg
We Invoke thee this Night:
Our Festival of Lights

O Divine Beings of Light
Ancient and Mighty Ones of the South
Keepers of Fire and Flame
Lend Us Your Power and Glory
Protect Us this Night of Imbolg

We Invoke thee this Night:
Our Festival of Lights

O Divine Beings of Light
Ancient and Mighty Ones of the West
Keepers of Water and Intuition
Lend Us Your Power and Glory
Protect Us this Night of Imbolg
We Invoke thee this Night:
Our Festival of Lights

O Divine Beings of Light
Ancient and Mighty Ones of the North
Keepers of Mother Earth
Lend Us Your Power and Glory
Protect Us this Night of Imbolg
We Invoke thee this Night:
Our Festival of Lights

The Invocation of the Trinity

Hail to the Ancient One - Genderless Spirit
We Request the Blessings of the three faces
Of the Holy Trinity
That Emanate from the Wonders of
Thy Vast Celestial Realm this Imbolg Night.

Hail to Our Glorious Lady Divine
Goddess of Infinite Understanding:
She who is today the Lady of Lingering Light
We Invoke Thee!
Hail to Our Wonderous Lord Divine
Our God of Infinite Wisdom:
Who Warms our Heart and Warms our Land
We Invoke Thee!
Hail to thy Blessed Holy Son, Jesus Christ,
Our Lord and Saviour:
O Scared Child
Of the Mother and Father
Tonight on this Festival of Fire
We Invoke Thee!

Statement of Purpose

Hail Brothers and Sisters!
We Gather Tonight on this February's Eve
For the Festival of Fire
And Purification
We Celebrate the Purification of the Virgin Mary
We celebrate the Mother aspect of the Goddess Brigid!

On this February's eve:
We call upon The Divine
Be With Us Tonight in our Worship,
Let all the Houses Be Ablaze with the Fires
Of Purification after a Long Cold Winter!
Let a multitude of white candles abound and burn
As the Young Solar God, Jesus
Ages and marks the Sun's return!

The Blessings of Brigid

We Banish the Winter
And we welcome the Spring
We leave behind what is dead
And welcome all living things!

Hail to Our Lady of Lingering Light
Our Most Beloved Brigid
We Look to Your Brightness!
Queen of the Candles
For purification they burn
On this very Night.

Within this consecrated area
Of Spirit and Light
In the sacred name of Lady Brigid
We begin this Rite.

This is the time for candles to burn,
For torches to glow and for every lamp in the house

To blaze in celebration
The purification by fire and praises to
Our Dearest Brigid
Holy Lady of the Lingering Light!

The Purification of Mary

O Father God,
By the gift of the Blessed Virgin Mary,
Bless Us So that We May Also Feel the
Intercession of the Holy Mother Spirit

In this Time of Glory to the Virgin Mary,
The Earthly Mother
Of the Promised Son.
Then end has come to the 40 days from
The birth of the Christ child;
Let Us Fortify the Blessings of the Virgin Mary
And observed this day of
Purification.

She is Chaste. [Blessed Be!]
She is Holy. [Blessed Be!]
She is Pure. [Blessed Be!]
She is Clean. [Blessed Be!]
She is Virtuous. [Blessed Be!]
She is Glory. [Blessed Be!]
She is Blessed. [Blessed Be!]
She is Divine. [Blessed Be!]

Blessed Be to the Earthly Mother
The Eternal Virgin Divine
The Human Mother of our Lord Jesus Christ
Who Walked Mother Earth herself
Mother Mary, Truly Blessed Are Thou
Amongst all women!
Blessed Be! [Blessed Be!]
Blessed Be! [Blessed Be!]

Purification by the Elements

[Light the Altar Candle]
In the Spirit of Purification
On this Imbolg - Candlemas:
We offer this Symbol of Fire
With Bright Blessings to All Who Circle!

[Light the Altar Incense]
In the Spirit of Purification
On this Imbolg - Candlemas:
We offer this Symbol of Air
With Bright Blessings to All Who Circle!

[Sprinkle the Dirt or Sand on the Altar]
In the Spirit of Purification
On this Imbolg - Candlemas:
We offer this Symbol of Earth
With Bright Blessings to All Who Circle!

[Sprinkle Water on the Altar]
In the Spirit of Purification
On this Imbolg - Candlemas:
We offer this Symbol of Water
With Bright Blessings to All Who Circle!

The Divine Did Place the Elements
Earth, Air, Fire, Water
In Our Life
To aid us both By Day and By Night.

[Toss a Sprig of Evergreen into the Fire, preferably using evergreen left from The Yule/Christmas Tree]
As this Symbol of Winter
Is Consumed by the Fire
So Is the Darkness
Consumed by the Light!

Blessed Be the Trinity

Blessed Be the Holy Trinity:
Blessed Be the Mother, the Father,

And the Holy Son!
[Blessed Be the Trinity!]
Blessed Be to Our Lord and Our Savior
Jesus Christ on this Festival of Fire!
[Blessed Be the Son!]
Blessed Be Our Goddess, the Symbols Moon and Earth
Purification through Fire - Renewed and Rebirth!
[Blessed Be the Mother!]
Blessed Be Our God, the Infinite One
Father of Jesus Christ, the Symbol of the Sun!
[Blessed Be the Father!]
We Give Thanks for All the Blessings We Receive
We Give Thanks and We Give Praise
Blessed Be the Holy Trinity
As we feel the Divine Powers Raise!

Circle chant - Raising the Cone of Power

Blessed Be the Fire of Purification - The Blessed Light - Sacred Illumination
Blessed Be the Fire of Purification - The Blessed Light - Sacred Illumination
Blessed Be the Fire of Purification - The Blessed Light - Sacred Illumination

Releasing the Cone of Power

Now we release the Energy of this Sacred Circle
Into the World
To benefit those who desire Holy Cleansing
And Purification of their Hearts and Minds
Feel the Warmth of the Divine!
Blessed Be!
[Blessed Be!]

Time for Meditation and Reflection

Communion

Circle Fellowship

[Passing of the white candle]
I rejoice with my Circle gathered tonight
To celebrate Candlemas as I
Pass this white light:
(Personal desire or petition spoken here)

Parting Prayer & Songs

Closing Thoughts/Benediction

The Festival of Lights is Now Over:
The Celebration of Imbolg!
Candlemas has now Ended
Our Purification by Fire
Has Been Observed
As We Look Eagerly to the Coming of Spring!
May The Divine Sun shine
Upon the Blessed Mother Earth!

Thanking the Deities

As we humbly thank Our Dear Goddess,
Our Mighty God and Our Blessed Saviour
For Assembling with Us this Night of Imbolg
We acknowledge the Holy Trinity:
With the Fires of Candlemas!

We ask you to stay if you will or go if you must
In Your Holy Arms
We are always comforted
In Perfect Love and Perfect Trust!
Blessed Be!
[Blessed Be!]

Dismissing the Quadrants

We wish to thank the
Divine Beings of Light
Ancient and Mighty Powers Of the North
Who command Mother Earth
For being with us
As we Celebrate the Festival of Fire
Stay If you Will - Go if you Must
Hail and Farewell!
[Hail and Farewell!]

We wish to thank the
Divine Beings of Light
Ancient and Mighty Powers of the West
Who command the Waters of the Earth
For being with us
As we celebrate the Festival of Fire
Stay If you Will - Go if you Must
Hail and Farewell!
[Hail and Farewell!]

We wish to thank the
Divine Beings of Light
Ancient and Mighty Powers of the South
Who command Fire and Flame
For being with us
As We Celebrate this Festival of Fire
Stay If you Will - Go if you Must
Hail and Farewell!
[Hail and Farewell!]

We wish to thank the
Divine Beings of Light
Ancient and Mighty Powers of the East
Who command Air and Winds
For being with us
As We Celebrate this Festival of Fire
Stay if you Will - Go if you Must
Hail and Farewell!!
[Hail and Farewell!]

Dismissing the Circle

Ostara, the Vernal or Spring Equinox
Spring Kyriat: March 21

Ostara or Spring Equinox is a solar festival, in which day and night, and the forces of male and female, are equally balanced. As with Mabon, the emphasis is on balance of all things: male and female, light and dark, and for Christians - the death and resurrection - the symbol of death and rebirth. This is the first day of spring, which marks the adolescence of the Sun God and makes way for the lushness of summer. Ostara was the name of the Virgin Goddess of Spring in Ancient Germany. It immediately follows another Christianized Pagan festival, renamed as St. Patrick's Day observed on March 17.

Easter is the Christianization of the fertility celebration of Ostara. The symbols affiliated with this Sabbat and Holiday: eggs more than any other symbol celebrate Ostara. The word Easter came from the Teutons, which was closer in pronunciation as Eostre. This is a time of birth and renewal of all things. The eggs are also associated with the female body in terms of procreation; it is easy to see in this association in the root of the word such as estrogen.

The Easter Bunny had it origins with the legend of the Germanic Goddess Eostre. The small field rabbit wished with all its heart to please this Goddess. As a show of his devotion, he decorated the sacred eggs with bright colors and intricate patterns and then humbly presented them to his beloved Goddess. She was so pleased with the bunny's beautiful work, that she wished all of humankind to join in and share her joy! Since that day, the Eostre (Easter) rabbit has gone throughout out the world carrying out her wishes, and delivering little decorated gifts of life.

Other celebrations include spring festivals of wine as the Greeks observed Spring Equinox as Dionysia, after the Greek wine-god Dionysus or his Roman counterpart Bacchus; this marks the making of the year's new wine made from the grape harvest of last autumn. Wine can be added to the Christian ritual of Ostara by references to Jesus and the Wedding at Cana, when He turned the water into wine.

The colors affiliated with Ostara: pastels, yellow, pink, and greens.

Contents Needed for the Ritual:
The Altar should be in the center of the Circle of worship. The Altar cloths can be green and pink or yellow. Needed for the magickal body of

this ceremony are a package of corn seeds, a potted plant (preferably a white lily), and a basket of decorated eggs. The three white main altar candles symbolizing the Trinity.

Ideas for decorating the Circle of Worship include cut flowers such as daffodils, lilies, and the early wildflowers. Adorn the Circle with plenty of pastel candles (even marking the perimeter of the Circle), and baskets of eggs.

Pre-Ceremony Preparation

1. Purification of Self: a purification bath with Magnolia.
2. Attunement Tea: Dandelion
3. Anointing Oil: Lotus
4. Incense: Poppy
5. Semi-Precious Stones: Moonstone and Rose Quartz

Consecrate the Intended Circle

Casting the Circle

[Walk the Perimeter of the Circle Twice]
I conjure Thee O Sacred Circle of Power
To Protect Us from All Negativity
At this Perfect Place and This Perfect Hour
We Call Unto the Holy Trinity
For Health, Wealth and Prosperity
As Above So Below!

[Walk the Circle a Third Time and Say]
I call this Sacred Space Cast in Perfect Christian Love and Trust!

Assembling the Quadrants

I call Upon the Good Beings of Malkuth
Keepers of the Watchtowers of the East!
Elements of Air and Wind
We Summon and Stir Thee!
Attend this Circle and Guard Us
This Night as we Celebrate Ostara:
We Invoke Thee!

I call Upon the Good Beings of Malkuth
Keepers of the Watchtowers of the South!
Elements of Fire and Flame
We Summon and Stir Thee!
Attend this Circle and Guard Us
This Night as we Celebrate Ostara:
We Invoke Thee!

I call Upon the Good Beings of Malkuth
Keepers of the Watchtowers of the West!
Elements of Water and Intuition
We Summon and Stir Thee!
Attend this Circle and Guard Us
This Night as we Celebrate Ostara:
We Invoke Thee!

I call Upon the Good Beings of Malkuth
Keepers of the Watchtowers of the North!
Elements of Mother Earth
We Summon and Stir Thee!
Attend this Circle and Guard Us
This Night as we Celebrate Ostara:
We Invoke Thee!

The Invocation of the GodPair

Hail to Our Lord and Lady Divine
Who Are In Heaven, Blessed be thy Names!!
Please join us in our Celebration
We Ask your blessings, understanding, and
Your Presence to be Among Us Tonight
As we Celebrate Spring Equinox
Kind God we Invoke thee!
[Hail to Our God!]
Loving Goddess We Invoke Thee!
[Hail to Our Goddess!]
Blessed Be the GodPair
[Blessed Be!]

Statement of Purpose

We Gather Tonight on this March Eve
This Spring Equinox, To Celebrate Ostara,
And the Alpha and the Omega
Of Our Lord Jesus Christ
We ask The Divine to Be
With Us Tonight in our Worship!

The Vernal Equinox

Spring marks the time of all things a-new
The Wheel of the Year Turns On
We see the wonderous miracle and
The Signs of
The Creator all Around Us!
The Long Winter Sleep is over
And the Time to Plant and Grow Returns!

Magick is in the air as Spring Arrives
The Days Grow Longer and the Nights Grow shorter;
Blessed is The Warmth of the Sun
After a Season of Snow and Cold.

We Celebrate with Seed and Plant
We Celebrate with Root and Stem
The Blessings of the Lord and the Lady
And the Glorious Son
With baby chicks and fresh eggs
The signs of Life abound

Blessed Be the Trinity for All
The Blessings of Life
Bestowed Upon Us!
[The Leader of the Circle or appointed member should pass the packet of seeds, a plant (preferably a white lily), and the colored eggs around the Circle as the blessings are spoken.]

The Ostara Blessing

Blessed Be Ostara!
The perfect balance of day and of night

All things are equal:
God and Goddess
Sun and Moon
Death and Life
Dark and Light.

[Each person takes a few seeds to hold]
Blessed are the seeds
We toss to the ground
Bring forth our nourishment
For the next year around.

[Each person reverently passes the Lily]
Blessed is the Lily
A symbol of death
Which adorns this celebration
With it's whispering Breath

[Each person takes an Egg from a passed basket]
Blessed are the Eggs
Colored Beautiful and Bright
Symbol of fertility
And the Symbol of Life

With Our hearts full of homage
We Request the Blessings of the Trinity
As we celebrate
The Alpha and the Omega:
The Beginning and The End!
Blessed is thy Holy Son, Jesus Christ,
Our Lord and Savior!
Blessed Be! Blessed Be!

The Alpha and the Omega Kyriat

Easter marks the time of the crusifixition, the death,
And the resurrection of our Lord Jesus Christ.
He was born unto this world, lived and
Taught, preached the message Of the Divine,
He was crucified and died
He was re-born to ascend to Heaven.

I am the Alpha and The Omega
The Beginning and The End
Saith the Lord
Which is, and which is to be,
And which is to come,
The Almighty.
Blessed Be.

Hear now our wishes and Blessings we ask
That you might help us
Walk the Path of Righteousness
That we may Never Taste Death
Blessed Is the Saviour
The Divine's Holy Son
Reflected in Nature:
The Three Are One! Blessed Be!

Blessed Be the Trinity

Blessed Be the Holy Trinity:
Blessed Be the Mother, the Father,
And the Holy Son!
[Blessed Be the Trinity!]

Blessed Be Our Lord, the Beginning and End
Our Saviour and King, Forever to Reign!
[Blessed Be the Son!]

Blessed Be the Goddess, the Symbols Moon and Earth
Mother of Jesus Christ, the Virginal Birth!
[Blessed Be the Mother!]

Blessed Be Our God, the Infinite One
Father of Jesus Christ, the Symbol of the Sun!
[Blessed Be the Father!]

Thus, bring forth the Sun of Righteousness
For He is the Alpha and The Omega!

We Give Thanks for All the Blessings We Receive
We Give Thanks and We Give Praise
Blessed Be the Holy Trinity

As we feel the Divine Powers Raise!

Blessed Be The Mother
Our Lady Divine
[Kyrie Eleeson!]
Blessed Be The Father
Our Lord Divine
[Kyrie Eleeson!]
Blessed Be Jesus Christ
The Holy Son
[Kyrie Eleeson!]

Circle chant - Raising the Cone of Power

From Birth to Death - And Death to Eternal Life
Life is Born Again from That Which Dies!
From Birth to Death - And Death to Eternal Life
Life is Born Again from That Which Dies!
From Birth to Death - And Death to Eternal Life
Life is Born Again from That Which Dies!

Releasing the Cone of Power

In Perfect Love and In Perfect Trust
This Circle Does Now Release Our Energies
Into the World to Those Who Have Not
Yet Found the Peace of The Mother, The Father and The Son
Bless Their Hearts, Minds, and Souls
As we are Mindful of our own Many Blessings!
Amen - Blessed Be!
[Amen - Blessed Be!]

The Great Rite

Candle to Candle
Spirit to Flesh,
Male to Female
The Divine Husband to The Divine Wife
We Celebrate the Joining of
Our God and Goddess on Ostara
The Divine Brings of All Living Things
And the Symbols of Blessed Life

[Take the outside two of the Trinity Candles and together light the third candle in the Middle]

Time for Meditation and Reflection

Communion

Circle Fellowship

[This is a wonderful time for the Circle to join in the seasonal Festivities in a light hearted manner still observing their symbolic actions.]

Eating the colored eggs
(Symbolizing taking new life into their bodies)
Planting the Potted Lily
(Symbolizing death and returning to the ground)
Strewing the Corn Seeds
(Symbolizing new life to spring forth to sustain life)

Parting Prayer & Songs

Closing Thoughts/Benediction

This rite of Spring Equinox is now ended!
Ostara is Honored and Inspires Us with Hope
For a Prosperous Season Ahead
Jesus Christ Our Lord
Reigns eternal
The Beginning and the End!

Thanking the Deities

As we humbly thank all the elements, spirits,
Fairies and the Angels for being with us as
We Celebrate Ostara
The Time of Balance, Harmony, and Equality
Between the Lord and Lady Divine:
We ask you to stay if you will or go if you must

Blessed Be the Holy Trinity
In Perfect Love and Perfect Trust!
Blessed Be!
[Blessed Be!]

Dismissing the Quadrants

We wish to thank the Beings of the North
Those who command Mother Earth
For being with us
This Night as we Celebrate Ostara:
Stay if you Will - Go if you Must
Hail and Farewell!
[Hail and Farewell!]

We wish to thank the Beings of the West
Those who command Water and Intuition
For being with us
This Night as we Celebrate Ostara:
Stay If you Will - Go if you Must
Hail and Farewell!
[Hail and Farewell!]

We wish to thank the Beings of the South
Those who command Fire and Flame
For being with us
This Night as we Celebrate Ostara:
Stay if you Will - Go if you Must
Hail and Farewell!
[Hail and Farewell!]

We wish to thank the Beings of the East
Those who command Air and Wind
For being with us
This Night as we Celebrate Ostara:
Stay if you Will - Go if you Must
Hail and Farewell!
[Hail and Farewell!]

Dismissing the Circle

Beltane:
April 30 or May 1

Beltane, which falls on April 30 or May 1, is the festival that joins the male and female principles of The All to produce an abundance of nature. Beltane falls on the opposite side of Samhain on the Wheel of the Year. These two Sabbats are often considered the two most important rituals of the year, as they mark the beginning and the end of the great seasons: summer and winter.

The ritual of Beltane is the symbolic uniting of the two as twin halves of a whole; take care to carry out this ceremony of cosmic procreation with dignity and respect to all of the members in the Circle. The Celestial Couple are the GodPair, the dual reflections of The Almighty, the One, the All - the creative Spirit behind the essence of the universe. The Celestial Bride and The Celestial Bridegroom are Our Heavenly Mother and Our Heavenly Father, incapable of separation.

Beltane is one of the greatest Celtic solar festivals, celebrated in ancient times with bonfires; the bonfires mark the occasion so greatly that some Wiccans call all Circle fires "balefires" throughout the year. The rites celebrate birth, fertility, and the blossoming of all life, as personified by the union of the Goddess and the Sun God, also known in Christianized lore as King Winter and Queen May. Folk traditions show celebrants jumping over broomsticks, (a fertility, or matrimonial symbol) and dancing around maypoles.

The sabbat begins at moonrise on Beltane Eve. Supposedly, it is bad luck to be out late that night because witches and fairies roam the countryside in great numbers and conduct wild revelries. Practitioners of the Old Religion believe the bonfires of Beltane brought fertility and prosperity to crops, homes, and livestock. It did indeed, because scattering the ashes from the Beltane fires over the fields acted as a fertilizer by enriching the soil. People dance deosil, or clockwise, around the fires or creep between the fires for protection against illness. At one time, farmers drove their cattle through the fires for protection against disease by burning parasites from the raw hide of the animal. Ancient Druids lit bonfires on hills and uttered incantations.

Church services and processionals in the fields replaced the pagan rites when the Church Christianized the sabbat of Beltane. The priests then lit the ceremonial fires.

The colors affiliated with Beltane are red, green, white, and yellow. The symbols affiliated with Beltane are eggs, spring flowers, and the May Pole. Beltane is a time for butter churns, weaving flowered necklaces, head crowns or hats known as chaplets and weaving baskets: this weaving symbolizes taking two materials and intertwining them to create a third.

Contents Needed for the Ritual:

The Altar should be in the center of the Circle of worship. Since this is the Celestial Wedding, using all white would be a creative addition, with silver for the Goddess and gold for the God. A woven wreath of flowers serves as a crown for the May Queen. Of course, if at all possible the Maypole is erected and the streamers of red, green, yellow and white; the dancers weave the streamers in and out representing the Celestial Wedding of the Lord and Lady Divine. Adorn the Circle with plenty of red candles symbolizing love (even marking the perimeter of the Circle).

Pre-Ceremony Preparation

1. Purification of Self: a purification bath with Rosebuds and Pedals
2. Attunement Tea: Dandelion
3. Anointing Oil: Vanilla
4. Incense: Patchouli
5. Semi-Precious Stones: Sapphire and Bloodstone

Consecrate the Intended Circle

Casting the Circle

[Walk the Perimeter of the Circle Twice]

I summon and stir thee Ancient Powers Within
Ancient Powers without - O Sacred Temple
Surround us with your Magnificence!
Circle us with thy protective powers
Let the Divine Energies Swirl and Build
And Become One With Ours!

[Walk the Circle a Third Time and Say]
I call this Circle Properly Cast and Protected by The Holy Trinity!

Assembling the Quadrants

Hail to the Archangel Raphael
Keeper of the Watchtowers of the East
Messenger of the Divine
Keeper of Wind and Air
We Invoke thee Raphael
To Celebrate Beltane and
This Great Rite

Hail to the Archangel Michael
Keeper of the Watchtowers of the South
Messenger of the Divine
Keeper of Fire and Flame
We Invoke thee Michael
To Celebrate Beltane and
This Great Rite

Hail to the Archangel Gabriel
Keeper of the Watchtowers of the West
Messenger of the Divine
Keeper of Water and Intuition
We Invoke thee Gabriel
To Celebrate Beltane and
This Great Rite

Hail to the Archangel Uriel
Keeper of the Watchtowers of the North
Messengers of the Divine
Keeper of Mother Earth
We Invoke thee Uriel
To Celebrate Beltane and
This Great Rite

[Light the quadrant candles and the first and third of The Trinity Candles]

The Invocation of The Trinity

Hail to the Ancient One - Genderless Spirit
We Request the Blessings of the three faces
Of the Holy Trinity

That Emanate from the Wonders of
Thy Vast Celestial Realm this Beltane Night.

Hail to Our Glorious Lady Divine
Goddess of Infinite Understanding:
She who is today the Celestial Bride
We Invoke Thee!
Hail to Our Wonderous Lord Divine
Our God of Infinite Wisdom:
Who Is Today the Celestial Bride Groom
We Invoke Thee!
Hail to try Blessed Holy Son, Jesus Christ,
Our Lord and Savior:
O Scared Child
Of the Divine Cosmic Union between the Celestial
Mother and Father
We Invoke Thee!

Statement of Purpose

Hail Brothers and Sisters!
We Gather Tonight on this May's Eve
To honour The GodPair
As we witness and honour
Their Celestial Marriage
And Divine pro-creation!

Welcome All to this Night!
Blessed Be this Ceremony of Beltane
We Celebrate the Bridal Chamber
Of Our Lord and Lady Divine
The Male and the Female Twin Halves
Of the One!

The Holy Day of Sacred Marriage
The Holy Night of Sacred Union!
May Their Sacred Union Be Fruitful
The Manifestation of All of Creation.
Blessed Be Our Mother and Our Father!

The Holy Day of Fertility
On This Day, The Lady Divine is A Maiden

On This Day, Our Lord Divine is A Young Man
Unite in the Rite of Sacred Marriage
As They Again Become One
This is the Symbol of Nature
That Mates In the Spring
The Animals of the Forest
And All Living Things
The Crops of the Field
The Flowers and the Butterflies
The Trees and the Fern
The Beauty of the Greenery
The Wheel Continues to Turn
As the Heavenly Husband and Wife
All Things Come Into Being
All Things Come to Life.
In This Act of Love
We Celebrate the Divine

The Wedding Vows

[Vows of the Maiden]
My Beloved is white and ruddy,
The chiefest among ten thousand.
His head is of the finest gold.
His Locks are bushy, and black as a raven:
His Eyes are the Eyes of Doves
By the Rivers of Waters, washed with Milk,
Moreover, Fitly set.
His cheeks are as a bed of spices,
As sweet flowers:
His Lips like lilies,
Dropping Sweet smelling Myrrh:
His Hands are as Gold Rings
With the Beryl;
His Belly is as Bright Ivory
Overlaid with Sapphires

His Legs Are as Pillars of Marble,
Set upon Sockets of fine Gold:
His Countenance is as excellent
As the Cedars
His Mouth is altogether lovely:

This is my Beloved and this is My Friend.

[Vows of the Bridegroom]
How beautiful are thy feet with Sandals!
The joints of thy thighs are like jewels
The work of the hands of a Craftsman
Thy Naval is like round goblet
Which wanteth not liquor
Thy Belly is like wheat set about with lilies.
Thy two breasts are like two young roes
That are Twins.

Thy Neck is a Tower of Ivory
Thine Eyes are like glistening Pools
How fair and how pleasant art thou,
O love, for delights!
Thy stature is like a palm tree,
And thy breast clusters of grapes.

In my thoughts,
I will go up to the palm tree,
And I will take hold of the boughs thereof:
And thy breasts shall be as
Clusters of the Vine,
And the smell of thy nose like apples;
And the roof of thy mouth
Like the best wine for my Beloved,
That goeth down sweetly,
Causing the lips of those that
Are asleep to Speak.

[Reply Vows of the Maiden]
I am My Beloved's and
His Desire is toward me.
Come Now My Beloved
Let Us Go Forth into the Field
Let Us Lodge in the Villages
Let us get up Early
To the Vineyards
Let us See if the Vine Flourished
Whether the Tender Grape Appear,
And the Pomegranates Bud Forth:

There will I give thee my Loves.

The Mandrakes give a Smell
And at Our Gates are all manner
Of pleasant fruits,
New and Old,
Which I have laid up for thee,
O My Beloved.

The Crowning of the May Queen

[The Groom Places the Ring of Flowers of the Bride's Head]
My Beloved Bride
I place this Ring of many flowers
Colors of Our Creation
Upon Thy Head
My promise to Never Leave Your Side
And Never Betray Our Love Under
The Blessed Name of The One
We are Joined Now - Two has become One
One as we have always been
One as we Shall Always Be!

The Essence of Youth and Vibrancy
My Beloved Bride and Fair Maiden of Spring
With this Ring of Flowers
I Crown you the May Queen!

[The Bride takes the first candle and the Bridegroom takes the third of
The Trinity Candles and lights the Second Candle symbolizing the Union of
their Divine Essence]

Closing of the Wedding Vows

All Hail Our Lady Divine
Young and Fresh and Beautiful
As the Earth every spring
Praise and Honour to Our Lord Divine
In the Summer Warmth
That He Brings

But They Are One
Let Us Celebrate Every Day of the Year!
Blessed Be!

Blessed Be the Trinity

Blessed Be the Holy Trinity:
Blessed Be the Mother, the Father,
And the Holy Son!
[Blessed Be the Trinity!]

Blessed Be the Young Goddess on this Beltane Rite
Blessed Be to the Bride - As the Cosmos Unites!
[Blessed Be the Mother!]

Blessed Be Our God, the Youthful Bridegroom
Consort of the Mother - From which all things Bloom!
[Blessed Be the Father!]
Blessed Be Our Lord, Who Forever Reigns
Our Savior and King, as we Celebrate Beltane!
[Blessed Be the Son!]

We Give Thanks for All the Blessings We Receive
We Give Thanks and We Give Praise
Blessed Be the Holy Trinity
As we feel the Divine Powers Raise!

Blessed be the Divine
[Blessed Be!]
Blessed be The One
[Blessed Be!]
Blessed be the Triune God
[Blessed Be!]
Blessed be the Spirit of Old - Blessed be the Spirit of The All
[Blessed Be! - Blessed Be!]

Let Us Now Thank the Holy Trinity
For All of the Blessings that We Receive
We Give Thanks and We Give Praise
Blessed Be the Holy Trinity
As we feel the Divine Powers Raise!

Circle chant - Raising the Cone of Power

**Husband and Wife -The Only Begotten Son - The Divine Trinity
The Three are as One!**

Releasing the Cone of Power

**We now release this Love and Divine Energy
Into the world and direct it
Towards All Young Lovers
May they each be the Other's Beloved and
Each Be the Other's Friend
Blessed Be!**
[Blessed Be!]

Time for Meditation and Reflection

Communion

Circle Fellowship

[Dancing the Maypole and jumping Over Balefires, a time for Fellowship, Singing, and refreshments.]

Parting Prayer & Songs

Closing Thoughts/Benediction

**This celebration of Beltane has Ended!
May the grace and blessings of
Our Lord and Lady Divine
Let this Night of Divine Union
Go with us from this Night Forward!
Blessed Be!**

Thanking the Deities

As we humbly thank all the elements, spirits,
Fairies and the Angels for being with us
As we Celebrate Beltane
To Honour Our Lord and Lady Divine,
In this Observance of Holy Union:
We ask you to stay if you will or go if you must
Blessed Be the Holy Trinity
In Perfect Love and Perfect Trust!
Blessed Be!
[Blessed Be!]

Dismissing the Quadrants

We bid thanks to the Archangel Uriel
Keeper of the Watchtowers of the North:
The Powers of Mother Earth
For being with us
As we celebrate the Celestial Union
Of Beltane
Stay if you Will - Go if you Must
Hail and Farewell!
[Hail and Farewell!]

We bid thanks to the Archangel Gabriel
Keeper of the Watchtowers of the West:
The Powers of Water and Intuition
For being with us
As we celebrate the Celestial Union
Of Beltane
Stay if you Will - Go if you Must
Hail and Farewell
[Hail and Farewell!]

We bid thanks to the Archangel Michael
Keeper of the Watchtowers of the South:
The Powers of Fire and Flame
For being with us
As we celebrate the Celestial Union
Of Beltane
Stay if you Will - Go if you Must

Hail and Farewell!
[Hail and Farewell!]

We bid thanks to the Archangel Raphael
Keeper of the Watchtowers of the East:
The Powers of Air and Wind
For being with us
As we celebrate the Celestial Union
Of Beltane
Stay if you Will - Go if you Must
Hail and Farewell!
[Hail and Farewell!]

Dismissing the Circle

Mid-Summer, Summer Solstice or The Baptismal Kyriat: June 21

Litha or Midsummer is a solar festival, which is almost universally celebrated. In the European tradition, the night before was Midsummer's Eve was a time for great magick, especially for love charms. It is customary to pick certain herbs at midnight to bring protection against lightning, fire, witchcraft, disease, and ill fortune. Witches and fairies roam on Midsummer's Eve, as they do at Beltane; there is a bit of madness in the air. Great bonfires are lit to help change the course of the Sun in the sky; the rites resemble those of Beltane. Burning wheels are rolled down hills, and burning disks are thrown at the sun. The zenith of the power of the Sun God manifests in the flourishing of crops and livestock.

The Roman Catholic Church Christianized the Sabbat of Midsummer to St. John's Day in honor of John the Baptist. The colors affiliated with Litha: gold, green, and blue. The symbols associated with Summer Solstice are: Fire, Sun, the blooming of the Mistletoe, and Sun Wheels.

Contents Needed for the Ritual:

The Altar should be in the center of the Circle of worship. The alter cloth should be blue and white (the blue cloth being associated with the waters of blue for the Baptismal Kyriat and white for the purity of the Trinity). The altar clothes can also be blue and green (again the blue cloth being associated with the waters of baptism and green to celebrate the greenery of summer and also the Celebration of Saint John The Baptist, who is represented by green). The three Trinity candles should be white.

142

The Circle of Worship can we decorated with summer flowers, such as marigolds, and greenery. Adorn the Circle with plenty of green candles (even marking the perimeter of the Circle).

Pre-Ceremony Preparation

1. Purification of Self: a purification bath with marigold petals.
2. Attunement Tea: Lemon or Orange Tea
3. Anointing Oil: Lavender
4. Incense: Sandalwood
5. Semi-Precious Stones: Tiger's Eye, Jade, and Lapis Lazuli

Consecrate the Intended circle

Casting the Circle

Let us now call Upon the Natural Energies
Of Mother Earth and the
Celestial Powers of Heaven!
Tonight we cast and summon the Circle of Power
As we assemble The Sacred Temple:
Hail to the Holy Trinity to
Surround Us and Protect Us!

[Walk the Circle the Third Time and Say:]
I call this Sacred Space Cast in Perfect Christian Love and Trust!

Assembling the Quadrants

Hear Me O Ancient Ones
Guardians of the Watchtowers of the East
Keepers of Wind and Air
We Summon and Stir Thee
Aid Us in Our Magickal Workings
We Invoke thee
Bless Us This Mid-Summer Night's Eve

Hear Me O Ancient Ones
Guardians of the Watchtowers of the South
Keepers of Fire and Flame

We Summon and Stir Thee
Aid Us in Our Magickal Workings
We Invoke thee
Bless Us This Mid-Summer Night's Eve

Hear Me O Ancient Ones
Guardians of the Watchtowers of the West
Keepers of Water and Intuition
We Summon and Stir Thee
Aid Us in Our Magickal Workings
We Invoke thee
Bless Us This Mid-Summer Night's Eve

Hear Me O Ancient Ones
Guardians of the Watchtowers of the North
Keepers of Mother Earth
We Summon and Stir Thee
Aid Us in Our Magickal Workings
We Invoke thee
Bless Us This Mid-Summer Night's Eve

The Invocation of The GodPair

Hail to Our Lord and Lady Divine
Who Are In Heaven, Blessed be thy Names!!
Please join us in our Celebration
We Ask your blessings, understanding, and
Your Presence to be Among Us Tonight
As we Celebrate the Summer Solstice
Kind God we Invoke thee!
[Hail to Our God!]
Loving Goddess We Invoke Thee!
[Hail to Our Goddess!]
Blessed Be the GodPair
[Blessed Be!]

Statement of Purpose

Hail Brothers and Sisters!
We Gather Tonight on this Blessed June's Eve
So that we May Celebrate

In the Midst of This Summer Solstice
To Celebrate the Baptism of
Our Lord and SaviourJesus Christ!
Be with us our Celestial Parents
As we Honour Thy Son
In Baptism:
Be With Us Tonight in our Worship!

The Blessings of Summer Solstice

It is in this perfect time and this perfect place
That we are between the
Waxing Year - a time for planning and renewal and
The Waning Year - a time for reaping the harvest
Before the Time that Nature Sleeps.

Our Mother Goddess and Our Father God
Are at their most powerful time in Nature
We are part o the Holy Trinity
And the Trinity is within us!
Let us Give thanks for our Many Blessings!

The Baptismal Kyriat

This Night of Summer Equinox
We continue to Celebrate
Our remembrance and Honour
Of the Baptismal Kyriat.

The Ceremony of Observance is Today
But the Teachings and the Meanings of
Salvation thru the Holy Waters
Of Baptism Should Live in Our
Hearts, Souls and Minds
Every Day of the Year.

The Interceding of the Mother Spirit

Elizabeth and Mary were filled with the Mother Spirit.
The earthly Mothers of John the Baptist and of

Jesus Christ, Our Lord and Saviour:
These women were truly blessed among All Women
For the Message Bestowed upon Them!

Hail Mary, Full of Grace,
The Lord is with Thee:
Blessed art thou amongst all women.
Blessed is the fruit of thy womb, The Christ
Holy Mary, Mother of God,
Pray for us know in this hour of transformation.

The Messages of Gabriel

And Gabriel said unto Zachariah and said,
"Fear Not Zachariah for thy prayers have been heard;
Thy Wife Elizabeth shall bear thee a son
And thou shalt call his name John.
Thou shall have joy and gladness:
Many shall rejoice at his birth."

The Glory of John the Baptist

And John did baptize those in the wilderness
And preached the baptism of repentance
For the remission of sins.
He preached to them that there comes
One Mightier than I who's shoes
I am not fit to stoop and unloose.

I have indeed baptized you with water
But He will baptize you with the Holy Spirit!
Then Jesus did come from
Nazareth of Galilee, and was baptized
By John of Jordan.

And it came to pass
When the Lord was come up out of the water,
The whole fount of the Holy Spirit descended
Upon him and rested on Him and said to him:
My Son, in all the prophets was I waiting for you

That you should come and I might rest in you.
For you are my first begotten Son that reigns forever.

And if any accept the Gospel
Of the Hebrews, told by James, the brother
Of our Saviour says:
Even so did My Mother, the Holy Spirit
Take me by one of my hairs
And carry me away to the
Great Mountain Tabor.

Blessed Be the Trinity

Blessed Be the Holy Trinity:
Blessed Be the Mother, the Father,
And the Holy Son!
[Blessed Be the Trinity!]

Blessed Be Our Goddess, the Symbol of Moon and Earth
Through the Womb of Baptism all find Rebirth!
[Blessed Be the Mother!]

Blessed Be Our God, the Bornless One
Father of Jesus Christ, the Symbol of the Sun!
[Blessed Be the Father!]

Blessed Be Our Lord, Who Died on the Cross
Our Saviour and King, So that None maybe Lost!
[Blessed Be the Son!]

We Give Thanks for All the Blessings We Receive
We Give Thanks and We Give Praise
Blessed Be the Holy Trinity
As we feel the Divine Powers Raise!

Blessed be the Divine
[Blessed Be!]
Blessed be The One
[Blessed Be!]
Blessed be the Triune God
[Blessed Be!]
Blessed be the Spirit of Old - Blessed be the Spirit of The All

[Blessed Be! - Blessed Be!]

Let Us Now Thank the Holy Trinity
For All of the Blessings that We Receive
We Give Thanks and We Give Praise
Blessed Be the Holy Trinity
As we feel the Divine Powers Raise!

Blessed Be The Mother
Our Lady Divine
[Kyrie Eleeson!]
Blessed Be The Father
Our Lord Divine
[Kyrie Eleeson!]
Blessed Be Jesus Christ
The Holy Son
[Kyrie Eleeson!]

Circle chant - Raising the Cone of Power

Through the Waters of Earth - In the Spirit Rebirth
Through the Waters of Earth - In the Spirit Rebirth
Through the Waters of Earth - In the Spirit Rebirth

Releasing the Cone of Power

In this Perfect Time and In this Perfect Place
We release our Circles Energy
Through out the Earth and Space
May this spiritual rebirth finds its way to all
Who Seek a New Beginning, Peace, and Comfort
When joined in Baptism with our
Lord and Saviour Jesus Christ
Amen!
[Amen!]
Blessed Be!
[Blessed Be!]

The Great Rite

Candle to Candle
Spirit to Flesh,
Male to Female
The Divine Husband to The Divine Wife
We Celebrate the Joining of
Our God and Goddess
The Divine Brings of All Living Things
And the Symbols of Blessed Life
[Take the outside two of the Trinity Candles and
Together light the third candle in the Middle]

Time for Meditation and Reflection

Communion

Circle Fellowship

[Passing of the white candle]
I rejoice with my Circle gathered tonight
To praise The Holy Trinity as I
Pass this white light:
(Personal desire spoken here)

Parting Prayer & Songs

Closing Thoughts/Benediction

This traditional rite of Litha has come to its end.
May your Summer be filled with the
Warmth of the Sun and
The Prosperity Mother Earth brings!
May the Celebration of the
Baptism of Our Lord and Saviour
Go with each of you each day of our Lives;

Great is the Lord and Lady Divine!

Thanking the Deities

As we humbly thank all the Celestial Spirits,
The Divine Elementals,
The Fairies and Angels of Light for being with us
On this Midsummer Ceremony
To Honour and Acknowledge the Holy Trinity:
Lord, Lady and Son!
We ask you to stay if you will or go if you must
As we are always comforted
In Perfect Love and Perfect Trust!

Dismissing the Quadrants

We wish to thank the Ancient Ones
Guardians of the Watchtowers of the West
Keepers of Mother Earth
For being with us
During the Celebration of Mid-Summer
Stay if you Will - Go if you Must
Hail and Farewell!
[Hail and Farewell!]

We wish to thank the Ancient Ones
Guardians of the Watchtowers of the West
Keepers of Water and Intuition
For being with us
During the Celebration of Mid-Summer
Stay if you Will - Go if you Must
Hail and Farewell!
[Hail and Farewell!]

We wish to thank the Ancient Ones
Guardians of the Watchtowers of the South
Keepers of Fire and Flame
For being with us
During the Celebration of Mid-Summer
Stay If you Will - Go if you Must
Hail and Farewell!

[Hail and Farewell!]

We wish to thank the Ancient Ones
Guardians of the Watchtowers of the East
Keepers of the Air and Wind
For being with us
During the Celebration of Mid-Summer
Stay if you Will - Go if you Must
Hail and Farewell!
[Hail and Farewell!]

Dismissing the Circle

Lammas or Lughnasadh: July 31 or August 1

Lughnasadh is the first of the three great harvest celebrations of the Old Country: the Grain Harvest at Lughnasadh, the Harvest of Fruits at Mabon, and the Harvest of Game at Samhain. The first harvest marks the beginning of the waning half of the year and represents a time to put back the bounty of the harvest for the lean months of winter approaching.

The sabbat observes the great festival of games and dance, named in honor of the Irish Celtic solar god Lugh. The word Lughnasadh relates to the words meaning, "to give in marriage" and once was associated with marriage contracts. Nine months away is the next Beltane, the birth of summer and life. In medieval legend, this festival celebrates Lugh's marriage to the Goddess Eriu, "the Sovereignty of Ireland." According to this lore, a hag named Eriu is transformed into a beauty that personifies the land of Ireland. Beginning with the first harvest, a series of celebrations and thanksgiving rites are held to ensure the continued bounty of the crops for the coming year. Lughnasadh or Lammas is also known as the Festival of Green Corn, Ceresalia, Elembiuos, and the Feast of Cardenas.

Lammas, from Old English terms for "loaf" and "mass," is a Christianized name for an old Saxon fruit-and-grain festival designated by the early English church. The holiday celebrates the ripening of apples and winter wheat, the latter of which, according to tradition, is made into loaves and blessed in the church. Lammas Day also was a day to settle accounts. In Scotland, tenant farmers took their first grain harvests to their property owners (land barons) on August 1 to pay the rent.

The colors affiliated with Lammas: Red, Yellow, Gold, Green, and Orange.

Contents Needed for the Ritual:
The Altar should be in the center of the Circle of worship. The altar cloths can be green and gold, symbolizing the green of summer and gold for the oncoming harvest. The Three Trinity candles should always be white. The Circle of Worship can we decorated with late summer flowers such as grain stalks. Adorn the Circle with plenty of green and gold/yellow candles (even marking the parameter of the Circle.

Pre-Ceremony Preparation

1. Purification of Self: a purification bath with eucalyptus.
2. Attunement Tea: Gold Seal Root
3. Anointing Oil: Lilac
4. Incense: Frankincense
5. Semi-Precious Stones: Citrine and Peridot

Consecrate the Intended circle

Casting the Circle

[Walk the Perimeter of the Circle Twice]
I Call and Gather the Strength
Of the Holy Ancient Ones
To encircle us with your Powers
To Lead Us and Protect Us
During this Night's Celebration
We Summon and Invoke Thee!

[Walk the Circle a Third Time and Say]
I call this Circle Perfectly Cast and Protected by The Holy Trinity!

Assembling the Quadrants

Harken Unto Us
O Spirits of the East
Ancient Keepers of the Watchtowers
The Powers of Wind and Air
We Invoke thee
Bless us as we Celebrate

The First Harvest of Lughnasadh

Harken Unto Us
O Spirits of the South
Ancient Keepers of the Watchtowers
The Powers of Fire and Flame
We Invoke thee
Bless us as we Celebrate
The First Harvest of Lughnasadh

Harken Unto Us
O Spirits of the West
Ancient Keepers of the Watchtowers
The Powers of Water and Intuition
We Invoke thee
Bless us as we Celebrate
The First Harvest of Lughnasadh

Harken Unto Us
O Spirits of the North
Ancient Keepers of the Watchtowers
The Powers of Mother Earth
We Invoke thee
Bless Us as we Celebrate
The First Harvest of Lughnasadh

The Invocation of The Trinity

Hail to the Genderless Spirit - the Bornless One
We thank you for the Blessings
Of this Life and
We Request the Blessings of the Trinity
As we celebrate the first Harvest of Lammas
Hail to Our Luminous Lady Divine
Who is Queen of Heaven
And Shines Brightly in the Night Sky
We Invoke Thee Great Mother!

Hail to Our Lord Divine
The Father of the Universe
To be with us As We Circle In Union
We Invoke thee, Sovereign Father!

Hail to the Divine Son,
Jesus Christ, Holy is He!
Our Young Solar God who ages with the
Turn of the Wheel of the Year
We Invoke Thee!

The Blessings of Lughnasadh

Merry Meet to our Brothers and Sisters!
We Gather Tonight on this August's Eve
To Celebrate the First Harvest
To Rejoice and Show our Thanks
For A Bountiful Reaping of the Benefits
From all the hard work
That we have sewn this Summer
As we watch The Wheel of the Year
Turn On and On!

On this Day (or Night) we pause to Praise
Our Lord and Lady Divine
For the Bountiful Harvest and
The Glory of the Fertile Earth.

God has been good to us again this year.
The Sun has shown brightly onto the Fields
Brought forth are the grains
And the stalks are filled with ears of Corn!
Mother Earth has been fruitful to us again
This Year!

Glory to the Seasons

One Generation passeth away, and
Another generation cometh:
But the earth abideth forever.
The Sun also Rises, and the Sun Goes Down
And He hastens to His Place where He Arose!

The Wind Goes toward the South, and
Then turns around into the North;

It whirls about continually, and
The Wind returns again to its course.
All the Rivers run into the sea, yet the sea is not full!

The Place from where the rivers flow,
There they return.
All things are full of labor:
Yet, humankind cannot speak it
Humankind cannot see it
Humankind cannot hear it.
The Things that have been, is that which shall be;
And that which is done is
That which shall be done:
And there is No New Thing under the Sun.

Blessed Be the Trinity

Blessed Be the Holy Trinity:
Blessed Be the Mother, the Father,
And the Holy Son!
[Blessed Be the Holy Trinity!]

Blessed Be Our Goddess, Our Heavenly Light
Shine on us Mother - On this Harvest Rite!
[Blessed Be the Mother!]

Blessed Be Our God, Our Light by Day
Who Warms the Earth and Our Hearts When we pray!
[Blessed Be the Father!]
Blessed Be Jesus Christ, from whom all blessings flow
We Return bountiful thanks for all that grows!
[Blessed Be the Son!]
Blessed be the Divine
[Blessed Be!]
Blessed be The One
[Blessed Be!]
Blessed be the Triune God
[Blessed Be!]
Blessed be the Spirit of Old - Blessed be the Spirit of The All
[Blessed Be! - Blessed Be!]

Let Us Now Thank the Holy Trinity
For All of the Blessings that We Receive
We Give Thanks and We Give Praise
Blessed Be the Holy Trinity
As we feel the Divine Powers Raise!

Circle chant - Raising the Cone of Power

Father Sun & Mother Earth - Blessed Be the Harvest Birth!
Father Sun & Mother Earth - Blessed Be the Harvest Birth!
Father Sun & Mother Earth - Blessed Be the Harvest Birth!

Releasing the Cone of Power

Now as let us release this energy into our Circle
To benefit our Families

The Great Rite

Candle to Candle
Spirit to Flesh,
Male to Female
The Divine Husband to The Divine Wife
We Celebrate the Joining of
Our God and Goddess
The Divine Brings of All Living Things
And the Symbols of Blessed Life

[The Priest/ess or Circle Elder lights the outer two candles; then take the outside two of the Trinity Candles and together light the third candle in the Middle]

Time for Meditation and Reflection

Special Communion Preamble

To every thing, there is a season
And a Time to Every purpose Under the Heavens
A time to be born and a time to die;
A time to plant, and a time to sow;

A time to kill, and a time to heal;
A time to break down and a time to build up;
A time to weap and a time to laugh;
A time to mourn and a time to dance.
A time to Cast away Stones, and
A time to gather stones together;
A time for silence and a time to speak;
A time to love and a time to hate;
A time of war and a time of peace.

Communion

Circle Fellowship

[Passing of the white candle]
I rejoice with my Circle gathered tonight
To celebrate the harvest as I
Pass this white light:
(Personal desire spoken here)

Parting Prayer & Songs

Closing Thoughts/Benediction

This celebration of Lughnasadh is now ended!
We have returned the many thanks of
The First Harvest of Grain and Corn
As The Wheel of the Year Turns On.
May The Lord and Lady Divine Bless Us!
In Perfect Love and In Perfect Trust!
Blessed Be the Holy Trinity!
[Blessed Be!]

Thanking the Deities

As we humbly thank all the elements, spirits,
Fairies and the Angels for being with us this
Celebration of the First Harvest

We acknowledge the Lord and Lady Divine
This Ritual of Lughnasadh
We ask you to stay if you will or go if you must
Blessed Be the Holy Trinity
In Perfect Love and Perfect Trust!
Blessed Be!
[Blessed Be!]

Dismissing the Quadrants

We wish to thank the Spirits of the North
Ancient Keepers of the Watchtowers
Who command Mother Earth
For being with us
This Night of Lughnasadh
Stay if you Will - Go if you Must
Hail and Farewell!
[Hail and Farewell!]

We wish to thank the Spirits of the West
Ancient Keepers of the Watchtowers
Who command the Waters and Oceans
For being with us
This Night of Lughnasadh
Stay if you Will - Go if you Must
Hail and Farewell!
[Hail and Farewell!]

We wish to thank the Spirits of the South
Ancient Keepers of the Watchtowers
Who command Fire and Flame
For being with us
This Night of Lughnasadh
Stay if you Will - Go if you Must
Hail and Farewell!
[Hail and Farewell!]

We wish to thank the Spirit of the East
Ancient Keeper of the Watchtower
Who command Air and Winds
For being with us
This Night of Lughnasadh

Stay if you Will - Go if you Must
Hail and Farewell!
[Hail and Farewell!]

Dismissing the Circle

Mabon, Autumn Equinox or The Feast Kyriat: September 21

The Wheel of the Year turns once again; day and night, and male and female forces are equally balanced. Mabon occurs on the Autumn Equinox, which falls on or around September 21. This is the time for the second harvest. Mabon is the completion of the harvest, which began at Lammas.

This is the Traditional Wiccan Thanksgiving Feast. It was brought from Europe to America with the Pilgrims and however Christianized it may have seemed, its roots run deep to this Celebration of Mabon. Before the era of modern timekeeping, the peasants of Europe celebrated Mabon on September 25. Technology now allows us to calculate the exact day of the autumnal equinox.

At the time of the Autumn Equinox, the sun enters the Zodiac sign of Libra, perfectly symbolized by the balanced scales. It is no wonder that "Michaelmas," a feast in honor of the Archangel Michael, was chosen to represent this day of balance, as Michael is most often depicted with a sword in one hand and a set of scales in the other!

We celebrate The Feast Kyriat of Jesus Christ as he fed the ten thousand with five loaves of bread and two pieces of fish. The Miracle of this grand feast can fall on the American holiday of Thanksgiving or the traditional holiday of Mabon. This holiday is for celebrating the prosperity of the year's hard work; one does not have to be farmer to harvest a bountiful financial crop.

The colors affiliated with Mabon are brown, orange, violet, maroon, and gold. The Symbols affiliated with Mabon include grapes, wine and garlands, gourds cornucopia, Indian corn, and sun wheels. It is also known as the time of the Festival of Dionysus, Feast of Avalon, Alban Eifed, and the Horn of Plenty, the Cornucopia. This is the time of rest as Nature declines, preparing itself for winter.

Contents Needed for the Ritual:
The Altar should be in the center of the Circle of worship. The altar cloth can be orange and gold, or your choices of fall colors and symbols of Thanksgiving. The Three Trinity candles should be white.

The Circle of Worship can be decorated corn stalks, bales of hay, gourds and the horn of plenty. The altar can be decorated with wreaths and garlands made from dried grape vines. Adorn the Circle with candles orange, gold, and maroon (even marking the parameter of the Circle). Many celebrate by lighting fires within cauldrons (if used), or burning leaves to fragrance the autumn air.

Pre-Ceremony Preparation

1. Purification of Self: a purification bath with patchouli
2. Attunement Tea: Any berry drinks
3. Anointing Oil: Myrrh
4. Incense: Cinnamon
5. Semi-Precious Stones: Yellow Topaz and Amethyst

Consecrate the Intended Circle

Casting the Circle

[Walk the Perimeter of the Circle Twice]
I cast this circle round me times three
For health, Wealth and Prosperity
Protect all inside and let energy rise
In the Name of the Holy Trinity.

[Walk the Circle a Third Time and Say]
I call this Circle Closed and Protected by The Divine!

Assembling the Quadrants

Hail to the Elements
Of the Divine
The Building blocks of our existence
Keepers of the Watchtowers of the East
The Powers of Wind and Air
We Invoke thee

Bless Us
This Day of Thanksgiving!

Hail to the Elements
Of the Divine
The Building blocks of our existence
Keepers of the Watchtowers of the South
The Powers of Fire and Flame
We Invoke thee
Bless Us
This Day of Thanksgiving!

Hail to the Elements
Of the Divine
The Building blocks of our existence
Keepers of the Watchtowers of the West
The Power of Water and Intuition
We Invoke thee
Bless Us
This Day of Thanksgiving!

Hail to the Elements
Of the Divine
The Building blocks of our existence
Keepers of the Watchtowers of the North
The Powers of Mother Earth
We Invoke thee
Bless Us
This Day of Thanksgiving

Invocation of The GodPair

Hail to Our Lord and Lady Divine
Who Are In Heaven, Blessed Be thy Names!
Please join us in our Celebration
We Ask your blessings, understanding, and
Your Presence to be Among Us Tonight
As we Celebrate the Autumn Equinox
Kind God we Invoke thee!
[Hail to Our God!]
Loving Goddess We Invoke Thee!
[Hail to Our Goddess!]

Blessed Be the GodPair
[Blessed Be!]

Statement of Purpose

Greetings Brothers and Sisters!
We Gather On this Blessed Day
So that we may celebrate
This Day of Thanksgiving - Mabon!

The Blessings of Autumnal Equinox

The Days grow short and the Nights grow Long
As Nature Brings Color all around us
One Last Time before the Winter Sleep.

The Chill in the Autumn Air brings a new Feeling
As we sigh release from the Summer heat.
The Leaves of gold, orange, and brown
Fall to the Ground and Rustle beneath our Feet.

Our Children are back to School and the Season
Of Festivities is Now Beginning.
We stock up for the Winter from our blessings of
The Spring and The Summer.
We are part of the Holy Trinity
Just as the Trinity is within us!
Let us Give Thanks for our Many Blessings!

Glory to the Archangel Michael

Glory to the Archangel Michael
On this day of Mabon
We observe the Trinity of Celebration, Grace, and Balance!
Michael, help us to be thankful on this Celebration
Of Mabon - for the blessings of this year
And the Wonders of our life that we take for Granted.

Michael, help us to find the Grace of the Trinity within
Each of us and let us share with those who

Have not the material blessings and
Those who have a heavy heart.
Give them your guiding Grace.

Michael, help us to understand the Balances
Of Life, Nature, and our Existence upon this Earth.
Help us to Balance Light and Dark, Male and Female
Our Universe and Our Souls.
In the name of the Holy Trinity, Let us all give Thanks
Of this Joyous Day of Mabon!

The Feast Kyriat

This Day of Autumn Equinox
We continue to Celebrate
Our remembrance and Honour
The Feast Kyriat.

The Ceremony of Observance is Today
But the Teachings and the Meanings of
The Miracle of the Two Fishes and the Five Loaves
Should Live Strong in Our Hearts,
Souls and Minds
Every Day of the Year.

Jesus Christ gave openly of Himself to his followers,
To Strangers and to those who would rebuke Him.
Let us make this an Example
That no other should replace.

Jesus Feeds the Five Thousand

Jesus went forth, and saw a Great Multitude
He healed their Sick.
And Jesus said, "I have compassion on the Multitude,
Because they have been with me three days,
And have nothing to eat:"
Speaking to his Disciples, Jesus asked
"How many loaves have we?"
We have here but five loaves, and two fishes.
Jesus Said, "Bring them to Me"

And He commanded the Multitude to sit on the Ground
And took the two fishes and the five loaves,
And looking up to Heaven, He Blessed, and Brake,
And Gave the Loaves to His Disciples,
And his Disciples to the Multitude.
They All did eat and were filled:
And they took up the fragments that remained,
Twelve Baskets Full.

Libations for the Divine

[Hold up the plate of cakes or designated food item toward the heavens and say]
On this Joyous Day of Mabon, We Celebrate!
Let us Return our Thanks
To the Lord and Lady and Holy Son
For the Bountiful Feast and the Food, that Sustains our Bodies
Throughout the Wheel of the Year!
[Put a portion of the food on a separate plate as a sign of thanks and sharing.]

[Raise a chalice of wine or juice towards the heavens and say:]
Likewise on this Joyous Day of Mabon
Let us Return a Toast and Drink of Honour and
Thanksgiving To the Lord and Lady and Holy Son
As we align ourselves with the Heavens and Earth!
Blessed Be!
[Blessed Be!]

Blessed Be the Trinity

Blessed Be to the Father of Jesus Christ, the Only Begotten Son
Blessed Be to the Mother of Jesus Christ, the Only Begotten Son
Thus, bring forth the Son of Righteousness
On this Day of Thanksgiving!
We Give Thanks for All the Blessings We Receive
We Give Thanks and We Give Praise
Blessed Be the Holy Trinity
As we feel the Divine Powers Raise!

Blessed Be The Mother

Our Lady Divine
[Kyrie Eleeson!]
Blessed Be The Father
Our Lord Divine
[Kyrie Eleeson!]
Blessed Be Jesus Christ
The Holy Son
[Kyrie Eleeson!

Circle Chant - Raising the Cone of Power

Great Is the Feast - Blessed Are We - Divine are the Powers - Three Times Three
Great Is the Feast - Blessed Are We - Divine are the Powers - Three Times Three
Great Is the Feast - Blessed Are We - Divine are the Powers - Three Times Three

Releasing the Cone of Power

Let Us Be One with the Divine
Now, at this Perfect Time
And In this Perfect Place
Release the Blessings of Mabon without Haste
The Message of Thanksgiving We
Release to those less Fortunate than Us
We Send Prosperity to All
In Perfect Love and In Perfect Trust
Blessed Be!
[Blessed Be!]

Time for Meditation and Reflection

Communion

Circle Fellowship

[Passing of the white candle]
I rejoice with my Circle gathered tonight

Of Mabon to express these thanks:
(Personal thanks spoken here)

Parting Prayer & Songs

Closing Thoughts/Benediction

This rite of Mabon is now ended.
We are thankful for the many blessings
Of this Harvest and of Every Season
As the Wheel of the Year Turns Onward!
We express our thanks and devotions to
The Father, The Mother and the Holy Son
Who Have Given so much to Us:
Let it be A Lesson of Giving to Others
Through Out the Year!
Blessed Be!
[Blessed Be!]

Thanking the Deities

As we humbly thank all the elements, spirits,
Fairies and the Angels for being with us this Mabon
To Show Our Thanksgiving and Praise!
We acknowledge the Lord and Lady Divine:
We ask you to stay if you will or go if you must
Blessed Be the Holy Trinity
In Perfect Love and Perfect Trust!
Blessed Be!
[Blessed Be!]

Dismissing the Quadrants

We wish to thank the Elements
Of the North, who command Mother Earth
For your presence with us
On this Ceremony of Mabon:
Stay if you Will - Go if you Must
As we Stand Together in Perfect Christian Love
And Perfect Christian Trust:

Hail and Farewell!
[Hail and Farewell!]

We wish to thank the Elements
Of the West, who command the Waters, Oceans, and Lakes
For your presence with us
On this Ceremony of Mabon:
Stay if you Will - Go if you Must
As we Stand Together in Perfect Christian Love
And Perfect Christian Trust:
Hail and Farewell!
[Hail and Farewell!]

We wish to thank the Elements
Of the South, who command Fire and Flame
For your presence with us
On this Ceremony of Mabon:
Stay if you Will - Go if you Must
As we Stand Together in Perfect Christian Love
And Perfect Christian Trust:
Hail and Farewell!
[Hail and Farewell!]

We wish to thank the Elements
Of the East, who commands The Air and Blowing Winds
For your presence with us
On this Ceremony of Mabon:
Stay if you Will - Go if you Must
As we Stand Together in Perfect Christian Love
And Perfect Christian Trust:
Hail and Farewell
[Hail and Farewell!]

Dismissing the Circle

Samhain, Halloween, or Hallowmas: October 31

Samhain (pronounced "sow-wen") is an ancient Celtic festival that celebrates the end of the Wheel of the Year, marked by the death of the Solar God, and the beginning of the Celtic New Year. Samhain formally indicates the end of summer; Samhain literally means "summer's end." The

Druids, in ancient Ireland, once sacrificed to their deities by burning victims in wicker cages. In those ancient times, all other fires were extinguished and re-lit from the sacrificial fire. This custom continues in Ireland and Scotland, all fires in homes today; practitioners extinguish and re-light their fires from the main bonfires, but now safely and without sacrificial victims.

Samhain marks the third harvest and the storage of provisions for winter. On this night of the year, the veil between the worlds of the living and dead is the thinnest. Souls of the dead can come into the land of the living. It is during this time that Wiccans of all traditions find it easier to communicate with their deceased loved ones. As an offering of respect and remembrance, some Wiccans bake cakes for the souls of the dead.

Samhain is a time for eliminating weaknesses, when farmers once slaughtered the weak animals of the herd that may not to be able to survive the winter. This custom has evolved into the modern practice of ridding oneself of unwanted habits and weaknesses. The Rite of Paper and Fire transpires by writing the undesirable qualities on a piece of paper and dropping them into a fire. Symbolically, as the paper burns and disappears, so do the weaknesses of the individual.

All Hallow's Eve or Halloween is the Christianized name for the Sabbat ritual of Samhain. The modern custom of trick-and-treating may have originated from an old Irish peasant custom of going door-to-door to collect money, bread cake, cheese, eggs, butter, nuts, apples and other foods in preparation for the festival of St. Columb Kill. Apples are included in many rites, especially as ingredients in brews. Dunking for apples may have been a divinatory practice.

The colors affiliated with Samhain and Halloween are orange, black, and red. The symbols affiliated with Samhain and Halloween: carved pumpkins or jack-o'-lanterns, costumes of the dead (both ghastly and celestial), corn stalks, and bales of hay.

Contents Needed for the Ritual:
The Altar should be in the center of the Circle of worship. The altar cloth can be orange and black; black for the dead and orange for the attraction of the dead. The Trinity altar candles are black in reverence for the dead.

The Circle group can spend the day carving pumpkins, arranging for a bonfire, decorating the worship area in the colors of Samhain. This type of unity brings the group of practitioners closer on a personal level, as well as readying the sacred area for the night's ceremony. The Circle can be decorated with flowers of the late fall, seasonal colored leaves on the altar and making the perimeter. Pumpkins and gourds, corn stalks, bales of hay, and carved jack-o'-lanterns can adorn the circle and/or the altar.

Pre-Ceremony Preparation

Purification of Self: a purification bath anointing with Apple slices or oil.

Attunement Tea: Apple Cider Tea
Anointing Oil: Clove
Incense: Patchouli
Semi-Precious Stones: Carnelian, Obsidian, or Onyx

Consecrate the Intended Circle

Casting the Circle

[Walk the Perimeter of the Circle Twice]
I cast and create this circle of Holy Protection
In the Name of the Holy Trinity:
That it shall serve as the
Boundaries between this world and the Next
As we progress into the realm of the Unknown!

[Walk the Circle a Third Time and Say]
I call this Circle Closed and Protected by The Divine!

Assembling the Quadrants

Hail to the Guardians of the Watchtowers of the East
Angels, Messengers of the Divine
Spirits, Elements, and Powers
The Keepers of Wind and Air
We ask your breezy presence tonight
As apparitions are let loose
From the Ethereal Realms
Bless Us and Protect Us
This Night of Honoring the Dead
May All Be Joined with The Divine!
[The caller now rings a bell]

Hail to the Guardians of the Watchtowers of the South
Angels, Messengers of the Divine
Spirits, Elements, and Powers

The Keepers of Fire and Flame
We ask your fiery presence tonight
As Spirits Roam the Earth
From the Ethereal Realms
Bless Us and Protect Us
This Night of Honoring the Dead
May All Be Joined with The Divine!
[The caller now rings a bell]

Hail to the Guardians of the Watchtowers of the West
Angels, Messengers of the Divine
Spirits, Elements, and Powers
The Keepers of Water and Intuition
We ask your flowing presence
The Dearly Departed are Among Us
From the Ethereal Realms
Bless Us and Protect Us
This Night of Honoring the Dead
May All Be Joined with The Divine!
[The caller now rings a bell]

Hail to the Guardians of the Watchtowers of the North
Angels, Messengers of the Divine
Spirits, Elements, and Powers
The Keepers of Mother Earth
As the Ghosts and Imprints of Another Time
Move Among Us from the Ethereal Realms
Bless Us and Protect Us
This Night of Honoring the Dead
May All Be Joined with The Divine!
[The caller now rings a bell]

The Invocation of The Trinity

Hail to the Ancient One - Genderless Spirit
We Request the Blessings of the three faces
Of the Holy Trinity
That Emanate from the Wonders of
Thy Vast Celestial Realm this Hallow's Eve.

Hail to Our Glorious Lady Divine
Goddess of Infinite Understanding:

Wise Goddess Crone
We Invoke Thee!
Hail to Our Wonderous Lord Divine
Our God of Infinite Wisdom:
Wise Father Sage
We Invoke Thee!

Hail to Our Lord and Saviour!
The Aging Sacrificial One
Soon to Depart from this Earth
We Invoke Thee!
Be with Us as We Celebrate
The Day of the Dead!

[The Circle Members walk in Circle Clockwise and Puts pictures and mementos on the alter and each member picks up an Apple]

Statement of Purpose

Hail Brothers and Sisters!
We Gather Tonight on this Hallow's Eve
On this Day when the Veil is Thinnest
Between this world and the next,
Tonight We Celebrate on This Day of the Dead!

Tonight Our Circle Honours the Divine - The Holy Trinity,
Our Friends and Loved Ones Gone before Us:
We Honour You with Peace and Love!

Guide us and unite us with those
We love and dearly miss.
If it is Thy Divine Will, allow those
Who have passed to speak with us:
Be a Guide to us throughout the year!
Now with humble thoughts and Great Respect,
Let the ceremony of Samhain Begin!

Blessings of Samhain

Blessed Is the Season of Samhain
The Wheel of the Year Turns Onward!
We Gather this Night to Celebrate

The Nearness of the Spirit World.

Tonight is the blessed Night
Of all Nights of the Year
When the Veil is the thinnest
To our Loved Ones Departed from Here.

What is will be and what was will be,
All time is Here and Now
In the Sacred Circle of Worship.

As we say "Farewell to the Summer",
We feel Wintertime on its Way!
The Chill in the Autumn Air is Brisk as
Orange and Brown Leaves rustle on the Ground.

Our Children play their Halloween Games
As Ghosts and Goblins with
Jack o' Lanterns and Tricks or Treats!
Again, Holy Trinity Has Been Good to Us
As the Third Harvest ends.

Apple Star of Life Ritual

[This Ritual should be even more relevant to a Christian Wiccan than a Pagan Wiccan due to it's Goddess seeking aspect of Christianity and the fall in the Garden of Eden.].

The Apple symbolizes Hidden Knowledge
Found in the Garden of Eden
On the Tree of Life
As we seek the Truth and the Search
For being re-united with the Christian Goddess
The Queen of Heaven.

[Practitioners cut the apple in half sideways, not through the core, in order to reveal the 5-pointed star of Divine Knowledge. Pass the Apple around the circle as each practitioner respects the Hidden Knowledge and the symbol of the 5 pointed star and takes a bite]

For Wiccans the Star of Life Symbolizes
Earth, Air, Fire, Water, and the One Spirit

For Christians the Star of Life Symbolizes
The Five Wounds of Christ

On this night of honoring the Dead
We too symbolically take on the Hidden Knowledge
Of the Tree of Life.
[Cast the Remaining Portion of the Apple into the Cauldron or Bale Fire]

The Rite of Paper and Fire

[Take a piece of paper and let each member of the Circle write a negative quality about themselves, which they no longer wish to possess.]

We ask The Divine to help us that we may be cleansed
Of Any wrongdoing, Bad Habits and Mal-intent.
May our energies be reversed and
Used to praise the Trinity
Moreover, let it transform us for all to see.
"Igne Natura Renovatur Integra"
By Fire, Nature is Perfectly Renewed.
[Drop the Paper into the Fire]

[Construct a doorway with a black cloth to simulate the Veil
Between the Two Worlds or the Other Side. Low Candle light should
Illuminate the area behind the veil. A box of tissues placed
In this area would be a courteous idea since this part of
The Ritual can be so emotional for some]

Going Through the Veil:

Glory to the Souls Departed

Tonight as the barrier between the two realms grows thin,
Spirits walk amongst us, once again.
They be family, friends and foes,
Yet, we Celebrate for them and do not feel Sorrow.
Hear Our Prayers
Dear Mother, Father, and Holy Son
The past year slowly dies and the Harvest is over

Let Us Cast Away Ire and Cast away Pride
May the good come to pass and the bad be cast aside.

As we ask for Divine guidance and protection,
With the promise of a New Year,
May we have good health, good wealth and be of good cheer.

May Our Loved Ones long departed
Be Our Special Guides
From beyond the Grave and from the other Side.

Give us strength and courage,
And Knowledge Threefold,
To be diligent and fruitful, as you
Aid us to achieve our goals.

In every ending is a new beginning,
Just as every beginning has an end.
After Life is we find Death, and in Death
We Find Life Again.

Watch over our loved ones, and us
Both here and departed,
For tonight are joined together again for
Fellowship and celebration.
Guide us and protect us,
In Perfect Love and Perfect Trust
Tonight and throughout the New Coming Year.
Blessed Be! Blessed Be!

[Each member of the Circle takes turns entering the veil
Spending 5 to 10 minutes trying to reach a friend or family
Member who has passed on to the Other Side]

We return now to the World of the Living
And to all that is Right
As we emerge from the darkness into the Light.
We close the door to the ethereal realm
Leaving the spirits behind, we ask
The Holy Trinity to
Let them Live in Our Memory and Dwell in Our Minds.
Blessed Be!
[Blessed Be!]

Blessed Be the Trinity

Blessed Be the Father of Jesus Christ, the Only Begotten Son!
[Blessed Be!]
Blessed Be the Mother of Jesus Christ, the Only Begotten Son
[Blessed Be!]
Blessed Be Jesus Christ, Our Saviour and Lord, the Son of Righteousness
[Blessed Be!]
We Give Thanks for All the Blessings We Receive
We Give Thanks and We Give Praise
Blessed Be the Holy Trinity
As we feel the Divine Powers Raise!

Time for Meditation and Reflection

Communion

Circle Fellowship

[Passing of the black candle]
I rejoice with my Circle gathered tonight
To pay our respects to the deceased.
I pass this black light and honour my
[Person we choose to remember]

[If children wish to celebrate Samhain, now is a great time for Games of bobbing for apples and Halloween Celebrations
After this Rite with spouses and Family]

Parting Prayer & Songs

Closing Thoughts/Benediction

This Rite of Samhain is now ended!
Let us Close The Celestial Veil between the Worlds
Of the Living and the Dead!
As we return to our place among the Living
And those we have honored
Return to their Spirit World.

Let us Remember those Who
Have gone before us!
Blessed shall they always be!
[Blessed Shall they always Be!]

Thanking the Deities

As we humbly thank all the elements, spirits,
Fairies and the Angels for being with us this Samhain
To Honor Our Friends and Families Departed
From this Earthly Realm, but never Forgotten
We acknowledge the Lord and Lady Divine:
We ask you to stay if you will or go if you must
Blessed Be the Holy Trinity
In Perfect Love and Perfect Trust!
Blessed Be!
[Blessed Be!]

Dismissing the Quadrants

We wish to thank the
Angels, Messengers of the Divine
Spirits, Elements, and Powers
Of the North, who command Mother Earth
For being with us
As we celebrate the Ethereal Mysteries
Of Samhain
Stay if you Will - Go if you Must
Hail and Farewell!
[Hail and Farewell!]

We wish to thank the
Angels, Messengers of the Divine
Spirits, Elements, and Powers
Of the West, who command the Waters, Oceans, and Lakes
For being with us
As we celebrate the Ethereal Mysteries
This Night of Samhain
Stay if you Will - Go if you Must
Hail and Farewell!
[Hail and Farewell!]

We wish to thank the
Angels, Messengers of the Divine
Spirits, Elements, and Powers
Of the South, who command Fire and Flame
For being with us
As we celebrate the Ethereal Mysteries
This Night of Samhain
Stay if you Will - Go if you Must
Hail and Farewell!
[Hail and Farewell!]
We wish to thank the
Angels, Messengers of the Divine
Spirits, Elements, and Powers
Of the East, who command The Air and Blowing Winds
For being with us
As we celebrate the Ethereal Mysteries
This Night of Samhain
Stay if you Will - Go if you Must
Hail and Farewell!
[Hail and Farewell!]

Dismissing the Circle

Drawing Down The Sun: A Solar Rite

Drawing Down the Sun, the Solar Rite is an all but forgotten ceremony in Modern Wicca. Its purpose is the equivalent of Drawing Down the Moon. Just as a woman's body benefits from the cycles and ceremonies of the Moon at Lunar Rites, likewise Drawing Down the Sun can benefit a male's body.

As male practitioners can attend Lunar Rites and gain the advantages of the Goddess, female practitioners can attend and benefit from the Solar Rite energy of the God.

I am including this ritual and the emphasis on its observation in this book due to the requests and statements of a male Wiccan that I met early in my research. He took a great deal of time explaining his frustrations at the lack of emphasis on the male aspect of the Divine in Wicca today. He also mentioned that hardly any authors include the Solar Rite in their books, and there is no emphasis on the male practitioner except the book *Wicca for Men* by A. J. Drew. Since that time I have met many longtime practitioners of Wicca, and similar forms of the Craft, who have never performed the ritual of Drawing Down the Sun; more surprisingly many practitioners had never heard of a Solar Rite that was not a Sabbat.

Realistically, I would think Wiccans of all traditions would include a Solar Rite, each month, just as most Circles observe a Lunar Rite each month. A Solar Rite should take place on Sunday (named for the day of the Sun), preferably at Noon when the Sun is directly above the Circle, and at its greatest strength of the day. If the Circle desires to light a fire, place it in the midst of the Circle and set to blaze at approximately 11:00 AM.

This Ceremony of the Sun transpires in practice the same as all of the phases of the Lunar Rites, the Sabbats, and the Kyriats. The one exception is the thanking and dismissing of the quadrants, as well as the Father and the Son; however, do not release the circle at the end of the ceremony. At this point, the Circle actually widens to an area where the Circle members may bring in their families and have a cook out, play games and enjoy the warmth of the Sun, symbolizing the spiritual warmth of the Father and Son. At dusk or by 6:00 PM, douse the fire - this action dismisses the Sacred Temple.

My hypothesis for Drawing Down the Sun becoming a less important if not totally forgotten ritual is sense of rebellion that the traditional Pagan/Wiccan community feels from Fundamental Christianity. Fundamentalists see only the Triple Male, with no aspects of the Female Divine; as a direct result, many Wiccans fall directly into the pendulum effect and swing to the opposite with importance stressing only the Goddess. Both forms of worship exhibit spiritual unbalance. Worshipping just the Mother or just the Father causes a lack of spiritual balance within the practitioner and their goals fall short of being effective. Balance is the key to any form of spiritual wholeness.

Contents Needed for the Ritual:
The Altar should be in the center of the Circle of worship. The altar cloths can be yellow for the Father God and Jesus Christ, (yellow and the sun are usually represented by specialty candles) and orange, for attraction of our Lord Divine.

The Circle of Worship can we decorated with plenty of yellow and orange candles (marking the parameter of the Circle).

Pre-Ceremony Preparation

1. Purification of Self: a purification bath with musk
2. Attunement Teas: Orange Pekoe (Hot or Cold)
3. Anointing Oil: Patchouli
4. Incense: Dragon's Blood Resin

5. Semi-Precious Stones: Bloodstone and Jade

Casting the Circle

[Walk the Perimeter of the Circle Twice]
O Ancient Circle - the Sphere of the Divine
I summons and create thee!
Banishing all Negativity and Consecrating
All of the Energies Within:
Assembly thyself Solar Temple!

[Walk the Circle a Third Time and Say]
I call this Circle Properly Summoned, Cast, and Protected by the
Divine!

Assembling the Quadrants

Hail to the Powers of the East
Lords of the Watchtowers
Keepers of Wind and Air
We Invoke thee!
Come Into Our Circle and Bless Us
On this Solar Day of Worship
As We Draw Down the Sun

Hail to the Powers of the South
Lords of the Watchtowers
Keepers of Fire and Flame
We Invoke thee
Come Into Our Circle and Bless Us
On this Solar Day of Worship
As We Draw Down the Sun

Hail to the Powers of the West
Lords of the Watchtowers
Keepers of Water and Intuition
We Invoke thee
Come Into Our Circle and Bless Us
On this Solar Day of Worship
As we Draw Down the Sun

Hail to the Powers of the North
Lords of the Watchtowers
Keepers of Mother Earth
We Invoke thee
Come Into Our Circle and Bless Us
On this Solar Day of Worship
As we Draw Down the Sun

The Candle Light Ceremony

[The Priest/ess or Elder positions himself or herself in a benevolent
Position and begins to light the
Three candles.]

[The Elder lights the white candle for the male principle of The Divine]
   We Evoke Thee,
   Father in Heaven
   Come Be Among Us!
   He who is Wisdom
   Commune with Us Today
   As we celebrate you, our Lord Divine.

(The Elder lights the red candle for the child principle of The Divine)
   We Evoke Thee,
   The Only Begotten Son
   Come Be Among Us!
   He who is Mercy and Compassion
   Bless Us This Day
   As we celebrate you, the Sun of Righteousness.

(The Elder lights the black candle for the female principle of The
Divine)
   We Evoke Thee,
   The Blessed Shekinah
   Who Dwells Among Us!
   She who is Understanding
   Watch Over Us Today
   As we celebrate the Father and Son Divine.

Invocation of the Father and Son

Most Glorious Heavenly Father

Our Solar Lord Divine
Most Gracious Sun of Righteousness
With the Sun we do align
O God within Us, O God Without
How can we ever be in doubt?

There is no place where I may go
And not there see God's face, not know
I am God's vision and God's ears
So thru the harvest of my years
I am the Sower and the Sown
God's Self-unfolding and God's Own.

We ask of your presence
From Up Above
Come to our Circle of Worship
And Shower Us with Your Love

Charge of the God

I am the Radiant King of the Heavens,
I am He - Who bathes the Earth
With the warmth of my love and adoration
I am the Cosmic Seed of Creation
When I am united with My Divine Bride.

I am the thousand-named Son of creation.
Know that by all names I am the same.
I am the Triple Male
The Son, The Father, and the Wise Sage.

I am the spirit of the horned stag,
I am the endless harvest for all Humankind.
For without planting there can be no harvest;
without winter, there can be no spring.
I am the yearly cycle of festivals:
My birth, death, and rebirth.

I am the spark of life, the radiant Sun,
I am the giver of peace and rest.
I am the ray of blessings to warm the hearts

And to strengthen the minds of all who seek Me.

Drawing Down the Sun

We Prepare Now to Draw Down the Spirit of the Sun!
Our Radiant Father in Heaven
I summon Thee and Invoke Thee
Mighty God of us all.
The Symbol of Strength and Wisdom
The Manifestation of
Mercy and Beauty
Be With us this day of Solar Worship!

As we Raise Our Hands
We Feel the Warmth of your Divine Love
In our Fingertips - In our Hearts
And In our Soul.

We raise our hands toward the Sky
To feel your Heavenly Touch
We stand together in Praise
Our Father, Our Lord:
We invoke Thee to Descend upon this Circle
And Pour out Your Holy Light and Loving Grace
This Day - Fulfill Us
As We Draw Down the Sun!

Psalms of the Father and of the Son

Ever as I pass through the ways
Do I feel the presence
Of the Father and the Son
I know that in ought I do
They are with me,
They Abide in Me,
And I in them, Forever.

No Evil shall be entertained
For purity is the Dweller
Within me and about me
For Good Do I Strive

And For Good Do I Live.
Love unto all things.
So Be it, Forever.

Procession of Names

[The members should walk the Circle Deosil. The many names
Of the Mother are called one by one and honored by the entire Circle.
This can be executed as statements by the
Priest, Priestess, Elder, or leader of the Circle;
The procession of names can also be executed as call and reply with
The members of the Circle.]

Heavenly Father - Holy Son Divine
Known by many Names
We call for you:
Yahweh, Jehovah, Adonai,
El, the Logos and Jesus Christ
O Divine Heavenly Father
O Divine Heavenly Son
We ask that you dwell within us!
Bless us with your infinite Wisdom and Mercy
Guide Us and Guard Us
In Perfect Love and Perfect Trust.
Hail Yad He Vau He!
[Blessed Be Our Father]
Hail Jehovah!
[Blessed Be Our Father!]
Hail Jesus Christ!
[Blessed Be the Son!]
Hail Adonai!
[Blessed Be Our Father!]
Hail El!
[Blessed Be Our Father!]
Hail to the Logos!
[Blessed Be the Son!]
Hail to the Good Father!
[Blessed Be Our Father!]

Through these words we have uttered
And these names we have called
The Presence of Our Heavenly Father
And the Blessed Son, Jesus Christ

Dwells among Us!

Let us Adore Him
For He is Wisdom
Let us Praise Him
For He is Eternal Mercy!

Blessed Be the Trinity

Blessed Be the Father of Jesus Christ, the Only Begotten Son
Blessed Be the Mother of Jesus Christ, the Only Begotten Son
Blessed Be Jesus Christ, Our Lord and Saviour, the Son of Righteousness
We Give Thanks for All the Blessings We Receive
We Give Thanks and We Give Praise
Blessed Be the Holy Trinity
As we feel the Divine Powers Raise!

Circle chant - Raising the Cone of Power

Hail to the Father - Hail to the Sun
The Divine Trinity - The Three Are One!

Releasing the Cone of Power

Let Us Rejoice and Let Us Blessed
As we Celebrate the Sun on this Day of Rest
On this perfect day on this Solar Rite,
We Proclaim:
"Let There Be Light"

Time for Meditation and Reflection

Communion

Parting Prayer & Songs

Closing Thoughts/Benediction

This Solar Rite is now ended
Beloved Father we ask you to dwell within us!
Bless us with your Wisdom
For Thine is the Kingdom, the Power and the Glory!
Beloved Son we ask you to dwell within us!
Divine Sun of Righteousness
Bless us with your Mercy and your Beauty!
Guard Us and Guide Us
In Perfect Love and Perfect Trust.

Thanking the Deities

As we humbly thank all the elements, spirits,
Fairies and the Angels for being with us this Solar Rite
To Honour Our Heavenly Father and the Blessed Son,
We acknowledge the Lord and Lady Divine:
We ask you to stay if you will or go if you must
Blessed Be the Holy Trinity
In Perfect Love and Perfect Trust!
Blessed Be!
[Blessed Be!]

Dismissing the Quadrants

We wish to thank the Elements
Of the North, who command Mother Earth
For being with us;
Stay if you Will to Celebrate this Solar Rite!
[Blessed Be!]

We wish to thank the Elements
Of the West, who command the Waters, Oceans, and Lakes
For being with us;
Stay if you Will to Celebrate this Solar Rite!
[Blessed Be!]

We wish to thank the Elements
Of the South, who command Fire and Flame
For being with us;
Stay if you Will to Celebrate this Solar Rite!
[Blessed Be!]

We wish to thank the Elements
Of the East, who command The Air and Blowing Winds
For being with us;
Stay if you Will to Celebrate this Solar Rite!
[Blessed Be!]

Dismissing the Circle
[The Circle is Closed when the balefire is doused at dusk.]

Conclusion

By picking up this book, it is obvious that the unification of Christ, Wicca, and the restoration of the Goddess, is a path that has interested you. Perhaps you have been seeking a spiritual combination that feels as if it was right for you. Perhaps no one else understands the path you wish to travel. Perhaps others have discouraged you. You may have felt alone in your spiritual conflict, but trust me you are not! I hope that the reconciliation of Christianity and Wicca, as displayed in this book, will give you a sense of security in knowing that you are not alone; perhaps it will allow you a sigh of joyful relief.

While researching the Book of Light, I have received hundreds of ecstatic emails and letters from magickal Christians thanking me for openly addressing this spiritual path, which many have awkwardly been practicing for years. I want you to know that you were equally encouraging to me with your kind words and tireless support, without which this book would have never been possible!

I also want to give you some reassurance of the validity of your spiritual path as I have discovered that many Wiccans have secretly been acknowledging the Christian pantheon for decades, simply under the guise of the Goddess and the God, or the Lord and Lady. Many Wiccans have done this merely to be accepted among their magickal peers. Don't let any individual tell you that your spiritual path is wrong; if it feels right in your heart, then that is all that matters.

I hope that the Book of Light has been exactly what the name intends - to be enlightening! Jesus and the Christian God and Goddess are there for all who wish to commune with them in the Circle of Power. The elements and angels are there to protect us at the Watchtowers. They have been there for us all along, and we only had to look to behold the simplicity of their celestial love. The sabbats and esbats are a dedication and appreciation of that love - and as Christians, we have a couple thousand years of adoration to make up to our Queen of Heaven.

Now, let us break bread and drink the fruit of the vine
As we celebrate with the Lord and Lady Divine!
Blessed is Jesus - He Blesses Us Still
An' it harm none, do what ye will!
Hail and Farewell and Blessed Be!
Merry us meet, merry us part, and merry us meet again!

Glossary

Adept: An accomplished individual who is highly proficient in a particular spiritual, mystical, or magickal system due to serious study and application of knowledge.

Air: In most magickal traditions this corresponds with East, the color yellow, the mind, intelligence, and the archangel Raphael, the art of invention and creative imagination.

Abyss: The gulf or break between the realm of the Supernal Triad and the world in which we live in as diagrammed by The Kabballistic Tree of Life. This Abyss (often referred to as the invisible sphere of Da'ath) marked the fall from Grace in the Garden of Eden.

Adam: The first human creation; the name literally means the "red earth" or "first blood." Adam Kadmon is the prototype of all human creatures (male and female).

Adonai: One of the Kabballistic names for God meaning Lord; the name for the personal Deity within us or the Holy Guardian angel.

Ain: Nothing, the void

Ain Soph: The Primal Creative energy; the energy through which nothing becomes something.

Ain Soph Aur: Limitless light, the void beyond the known universe represented by the Tree of Life.

Anthropomorphism: The attribution of human features, personality, and/or characteristics to a Deity. These attributes are assigned for humankind's better visualization or understanding of a God/dess.

Assiah: The fourth world of material, of material manifestation, of humans, and of other manifest beings - our world.

Atzieluth: The first world of creative essence, the realm of Mother-Father Deity.

Akasha: The fifth element, the omnipresent spiritual power that permeates the universe. Also known simply as 'Spirit'.

Alchemy: A pre-cursor to science developed in the Middle Ages that sought to magickally and/or chemically turn base metals into gold.

Altar: A special, flat surface set aside exclusively for spiritual workings and/or religious acknowledgment.

Amulet: A magickally charged, protective, object that deflects specific, usually negative energies.

Ankh: An Egyptian hieroglyph widely used as a symbol of eternal life, love, and reincarnation. It is in the shape of a cross with a looped top.

Apocalypse: Literally "that which is revealed"; these were texts ranging 200 BCE to 200 CE popular to Christianity, Judaism, and Zoroastrianism.

Apocalyptic books were often written in secret or coded language. The theme of these books usually describes a dramatic end of the world.

Aspect: The particular principle or part of the Creative Life Force being worked with or acknowledged at any one time.

Astral Plane: A place that is generally conceptualized as an invisible parallel world that remains unseen from our own solid world of form.

Astral Projection: The process of separating the metaphysical aspects of the body from the physical body in order to accomplish travel on the astral plane.

Astrology: The study of and belief in the effects the movements and placements of planets and other heavenly bodies have on the lives and behavior of human beings.

Athame: (a-tha-may) The sacred black handled knife used in Wiccan rituals. Used for the directing and re-directing of energies, the athame is a symbolic pointer: it is not used for cutting. This is traditionally a double-edged knife with a leaf-shaped blade. Depending on the tradition followed, it is a symbol for either Air or Fire. The term is of obscure origin, has many variant spellings, and an even greater variety of pronunciations. Pronounced "Ah-THAM-ee" (which would rhyme with "whammy), "ATH-ah-may," or "ah-THAW-may."

Attunement: An activity, which brings the minds, emotions, and psyches of a group into harmony before ritual: chanting, singing, guided meditation, and breathing exercises are common ways to attune.

Aura: The energy field of the human body. Specifically, the aura is the radiant energy portion visible to the third eye or psychic vision. The aura can reveal information about an individual's health and emotional state.

Balefire: A fire lit usually outdoors, especially equated with the Sabbats of Yule, Beltane, and Midsummer.

Bane: That which destroys life. It is poisonous, destructive, and dangerous.

Banish: To end a specific set of activities or to exorcise unwanted entities. The method of ridding a particular space or area of unwanted energies.

B.C.E.: Before Common Era. Synonymous with B.C.E. or Before Christ, but without religious bias.

Bell: A ritual tool associates with angel workings and elemental invocations. Bells can invoke directional energies or cleanse a space. Bells are associated with the element of Air and mark the end of some festivals such as Beltane.

Beltane: A Wiccan festival celebrated on April 30th or May 1st (traditions vary). Beltane is also known as May Eve, May Day, Roodmas, Walpurgis Night, and Cethsamhain. Beltane celebrates the symbolic union, mating, or marriage of the Goddess and God, and links in with the approaching summer months.

Bolline: The white-handled knife used in many traditions of Wicca. It is used for carving or cutting materials that are necessary for rituals, medicines, or spells. It is also used for harvesting herbs and has a small silver sickle shaped blade.

Book of Light: This is the Christian Wiccan's magickal journal and the contents vary from practitioner to practitioner. Most contain information about the festivals of the year, ceremonies, prayers, and statements of spiritual empowerment. It contains information about working with the Judeo-Christian Trinity, angels, and the saints. Herbal recipes, the charkas, color and aromatherapy and healing gem therapy is also helpful. If written as a heirloom, it is important to journal the debunking of superstitions about Wicca, the pentacle, and the fact of non-Satanic associations.

Book of Shadows: (also known as The Book of Shadows and Light). It is a pagan Wiccan's magickal journal of rituals, spells, dreams, herbal recipes, magickal lore etc. It is called the BOS for short; no one "true" Book of Shadows exists; all are relevant to their respective users.

Burning Times: The name given to a historical time around 1000 C.E. through the 17th century when many people were tortured and burned by church and public officials on the assumption that they were the Christian version of Witches. This turned into an extremely profitable venture, as all land and property was seized from the accused individual and portions given to the accuser (as a reward) and the remainder seized by the church officials.

Cabala - (see Kabbalah)

Cakes and Ale: The Wiccan "communion" that consists of a natural beverage and cake offered to each participant in a ritual, or eaten by participants at the end of the ritual as a part of the grounding process.

Call (to Call): To Invoke the Divine, The Trinity, the Archangels, angels, the elemental forces and energies.

Casting Stones: A form of divination where one throws small stones on the ground or a special board or cloth. These stones may be marked with runes, or their color may indicate their meaning. Also called Lithomancy.

Casting the Circle: The psychic creation of a sphere of energy around the area where a ritual is to be performed; both to concentrate and focus the power raised and to keep out unwanted influences or distractions. The space enclosed exists outside of ordinary space and time.

C.E.: the Common Era. Synonymous with A.C.E., but without religious bias.

Censer: A heatproof container in which incense is burned; it is associated with the element of air.

Centering: The process of moving one's consciousness to one's spiritual center; leading to a feeling of great peace, calmness, strength, clarity and stability.

Chakras: Seven major energy vortexes found in the human body, which pass psychic and elemental energies. Each is usually associated with a color.

Chant: This is usually a rhyme intoned rhythmically to raise power. Chants which rhyme can be simple and repetitive; it makes them easier to remember and it always one's mind to multi-task.

Chaplet: A circlet for the head usually made of flowers and worn at Beltane or during a hand fasting.

Charging: Infusing an object with personal power.

Charm: An amulet or talisman that has been charged and energized for a specific task.

Chesed: Mercy, love, and the fourth sephirah, relating to Chockmah: Wisdom, the second sephirah, relating to the Father God. The sphere associated with spiritual purpose.

Circle: Sacred space wherein all rituals and worship ceremonies are to be contained. It both holds ritual energy until the practitioner is ready to release it, and provides protection for the Wiccan.

Cleansing: Ritualistically removing negative energies from an object or space, using water and various cleansing materials. Cleansing can also be achieved by focusing your personal power behind the demand for all negative energies to leave a polluted area.

Collective Unconsciousness: Term used to describe the sentient connection of all living things, past and present. Jungian theories are heavily based in the collective unconsciousness and synchronicity; may also be called the Akashic Records.

Compartmentalization: Cone of Power: Psychic energy raised and focused within a Circle, directed to achieve a definite purpose or achieve a collective goal.

Conscious Mind: The analytical, materially based, rational half of our consciousness. The part of our mind that is at work while we balance our checkbooks, theorize, communicate, and perform other acts related to the physical world.

Consecration: The act of blessing an object or place by instilling it with positive energy for sacred purposes.

Corn Dolly: A figure, often human-shaped, created by plaiting dried wheat or other grains. The doll represents the fertility of the Earth and the Goddess in early European agricultural rituals; it is still used in Wicca. Corn dollies aren't made from cobs or husks but from wheat or other grains; corn originally referred to any grain other than maize and still does in most English-speaking countries, except the United States.

Cross-Quarter Days: Refers to Sabbats falling on the solstices or equinoxes.

Cult: A group that professes spiritual in nature, but requires a great deal of energy and/or money from its followers as 'proof' of their devoutness; frequently dependent on the charisma of a Leader. Cults are frowned upon by all Wiccan traditions, because the uneducated person usually confuses a cult with a circle.

Da'ath: Knowledge, the eleventh sephirah, or the sphere without number. The gateway to hidden knowledge

Days of Power: Days triggered by astrological occurrences, sabbats, moon cycles. Other special events may include your birthday, your menstrual cycle, your baptism, initiation anniversary, etc.

Deity: A God or Goddess.

Deosil: (pronounced "juh-sil") Clockwise, the direction in which the shadow on a sundial moves as the Sun "moves" across the sky. Deosil has been through superstitions (see Widdershins) most commonly associated as automatically positive: positive energies and positive energies.

Divination: The self-introspective art of discovering the unknown by interpreting random patterns or symbols through the use of tools such as clouds, tarot cards, flames, and smoke. Divination contacts the Psychic Mind by drowsing the Conscious Mind through ritual and observation or of manipulation of tools.

Divine Power: The pure energy that exists and exudes from the Divine or the Holy Trinity; the life force, the ultimate source of all things.

Drawing Down the Moon: A lunar rite performed during the full moon by all traditions of Wicca for empowerment, to re-affirm one's self-dedication and to unite their essence with the Goddess, the Mother God, or the Lady Divine.

Drawing Down the Sun: A solar rite, a lesser known and lesser used companion ritual to Drawing Down the Moon rarely used by many traditions of Wicca. However, Trinitarian or Christian Wiccans observe this ritual once a month on a sunny weekend day usually lasting from 11 AM until 6:00 PM (please avoid sunburn). This is a festival day in which the essence of the Father God and Jesus Christ are the empowering forces as the paternal part of the Trinity.

Duality: The opposite of polarity. When used as a religious term, it separates two opposites such as good and evil and places those characteristics into two completely separate and opposite Deity forms, i.e. God and Satan.

Earth: In most traditions, the element corresponds to the North; the colors green is most noted for quadrant candles, while other colors include the Kaballistic black association as well as brown depicting woodland and soil. Earth is associated with foundation, stability, the human body, all solid material things, and prosperity.

Earthing: Also known as grounding, this is the act of sending excess energy into the Earth. It can be done any time residual power has a surplus for any number of reasons; earthing and grounding at this time is a pro-health act.

Earth Power: The energy that exists within stones, herbs, flames, wind, and other natural objects.

Eclectic: Selecting or made up of what seems best of varied sources.

Eden: The Garden of Unity to which we return when we realize union with the Divine, here on earth.

Elohim: Usually translated as God. Alternate translations include the Mother-Father Deity. The word is composed of a feminine singular with a masculine plural, thus expressing the unity of both male and female principles.

Elder: One who is recognized as an experienced leader, teacher, and counselor within the Trinitarian Circle.

Elements: Usually: earth, air, fire, water, they are the building blocks of the universe. Everything that exists contains one or more of these energies. Some include a fifth element - The One Spirit, Akasha, The High God, The All or YHWH.

Elementals: Archetypal spirit beings associated with one of the four elements.

Equinox: Either of the two times each year (as about March 21 and September 23) when the sun crosses the equator and day and night are of equal length.

Esbat: A ritual occurring on the New or Full Moon and dedicated to the Goddess in her lunar aspect. It derives from the French word esbattre, which means, "to frolic."

Esoteric: Specific spiritual ideas, literature, and doctrines intended for and only understood by a select group of individuals, disciples, or followers

Eve: The first woman. The inner aspect of all humans (male and female) through which we come to know ourselves.

Evocation: To call a spirit, deity or elemental into the practitioner's immediate presence.

Fire: In many traditions, the element corresponds to the South, the color red, energy, will, passion, determination, purpose, ambition, and spirituality.

First Quarter: One half of the Moon appears illuminated by direct sunlight while the illuminated part is increasing

Folklore: Traditional sayings, cures, wisdom of a particular locale which is separate from their mythology.

Folk Magick: The practice of projecting personal power, as well as the energies within natural objects such as herbs, home remedies and crystals, to bring about needed changes.

Full Moon: The Moon fully illuminated by direct sunlight.

Geburah: Strength, judgment, and the fifth sephirah relating to

Gematria: Kabballistic numerological system where words having the same numerical value are said to be essentially identical. A meditation or technique for attaining enlightenment.

Gnosis: Greek term; a type of personal spiritual knowledge obtained directly from the Divine by methods of meditation and self-introspection.

Gnosticism: The modern term used to describe various groups seeking spiritual enlightenment through personal revelation or gnosis.

Gnostics: Seekers of gnosis in the Hellenistic period, including Pagans, Jews, and Christians.

Gnostic Christians: The mystic Christians who sought direct spiritual enlightenment from the Living Jesus, the Good Father, and the Goddess Sophia during the late Hellenistic period.

God: The masculine aspect of The Divine One Spirit.

Goddess: The feminine aspect of The Divine One Spirit.

Great Law: As written by respected Wiccan literary Dion Fortune "All Gods are the Same God and All Goddesses are the Same Goddess", in turn making up the One Genderless Spirit.

Great Rite: Symbolic union or the sacred marriage of the male (Lord Divine) and female (Lady Divine) aspect of The All or the High God that is generally enacted at Beltane in many traditions. It symbolizes the primal act of creation from which all life comes.

Great Work: An alchemical term summarized in the words of Jesus: "know thyself"

Grounding and/or Centering: The process of connecting oneself to the Earth (grounding) and aligning one's own energy flow.

Guardians: The beings, creatures, or angels that protect the four quadrants and command the elements within the Circle.

Hod: Splendor, the eighth sephirah, related to the sphere of thinking.

Healing: The goal of a great deal of earth magick, especially among many Wiccan traditions, is healing. Some alternative forms of healing include chakra/energy work, visualization, herb craft, crystal/gem/metal healing, color, and aromatherapy.

Heathen: A modern slanderous term for a non-Christian. Originally, the term indicated "one who dwells on the heath."

Herb: A plant or plant part valued for its medicinal, savory, or aromatic qualities. An herbalist refers to the practitioner of the art and the art itself of working with herbs to facilitate human needs, most often time in regards to healing and medicine.

Higher Self: That part of us that connects our corporeal minds to the Collective Unconscious and with the Divine knowledge of the universe.

Horned God: One of the most prevalent God-images in Paganism. In Christian (Trinitarian and/or Esoteric) Wiccan's defense of the Pagans, despite much Christian fundamentalist's propaganda, this is not Satan. Instead, he is the God of the Harvest, and the horns are horns of plenty or cornucopias, still used in Christian Thanksgiving symbolism.

Imbolc: A Wiccan festival celebrated on February 2, also known as Candlemas, Lupercalia, the Feast of Troches, the Festival of Lights, Oimelc, Brigit's Day, and many other names. Imbolc celebrates the first stirrings of spring, Hail to Sainte Brigit, and the Purification of Mary.

Immanence: belief or experience that The Divine is already manifesting in all things and is to be found within. The way of the Kabbalah is essentially biased toward immanence.

Incense: Ritual burning of herbs, oils, or other aromatic items to scent the air during acts of magick and ritual, and helps the witch attune to the goal of the working. A symbol of Fire and Air, they may be in the form of sticks, cones, resins, or dried herbs. The incense chosen will depend on the nature of the worship ceremony or simply because of what works best for each individual.

Initiate: Someone who has been through a Ritual of Initiation, and taken vows to study and dedicate oneself to the Holy Trinity. They vary a bit from group to group. As Trinitarians, initiation to the Circle is followed after baptism.

Initiation: A ritual during which an individual is introduced or admitted into a regular worship Circle.

Invocation: To bring something in from without. An appeal or petition to a higher power (or powers), such as Our Divine Goddess and God, the Archangels, the elements, spirits, saints, or other celestial powers. This is in the form of a prayer. Invocation is actually a method of establishing conscious ties with those aspects of the Goddess and God that dwell within us. In essence, then, we seemingly cause them to appear or make themselves known by becoming aware of them.

Kabbalah: Mystical Jewish teaching system; the word literally translates "that which is received." Ceremonial Magick, the High Magick of the Golden Dawn, as well as the Alexandrian, and Trinitarian Wicca traditions are based in these teachings. The system by which knowledge of The Divine is revealed. A practical system for Divine Revelation, understanding ourselves, our world, especially in direct regard to the one-on-one personal affiliation with The Trinity.

Karma: The belief that one's thoughts and deeds can either be counted against them or added to their spiritual path across several life times.

Kether: the Crown, the first Sephirah related to the High Spirit. This sphere transmits the influence from the trans-mundane realms towards the earth.

Lady Divine: The female aspect of The All, Our Heavenly Mother, or the Christian Goddess, representing motherhood, mid-life, and fertility. She is represented by the full moon, the egg, the earth, water, and the colors red and green. We refer to Her by any of the names of Her aspects. She is all encompassing, containing especially all creative and procreative properties, all aspects of nurturing and healing, all forms of birth and rebirth, all growth and plenty. All women partake of Her nature, and are part of Her. To Christian Wiccans, the Lord and the Lady Divine bring forth all the life that is on the earth, including their Blessed Son, our Saviour Jesus Christ.

Last Quarter: One-half of the moon appears to be illuminated by direct sunlight while the illuminated part is decreasing.

Law of Return: Whatever energy is sent out returns to the sender multiplied. Some traditions say it is multiplied by three, and therefore call this principle the "Threefold Law."

Left-Hand Path: The practice of using magick to control others, to change the will of others, and for personal gain. Types of magick considered unethical and generally frowned upon.

Libation: A ritually given portion of food or drink to a Deity, spirit or nature, or being from another realm.

Lord Divine: Our Heavenly Father, Our God. We refer to Him by the names of His aspects. He is the Lord of Birth, Life, Death, and Resurrection. He is the Consort of the Lady Divine. He is sensuality, strength, music, and lust. All men partake of His nature, and are part of Him. He is the sun, the sky, and the wind. Together, the Lord and the Lady Divine bring forth all the life that is on the earth.

Lughnasadh: A Wiccan festival celebrated on August 1, also known as August Eve, Lammas, Feast of Bread. Lughnasadh marks the first harvest, when the fruits of the Earth are cut and stored for the dark winter months, and when the days grow shorter.

Lunar Cycle: Roughly a 29-day cycle during which the visible phase of the Moon waxes from dark to full and wanes to dark again.

Mabon: On or around September 21, the Autumn Equinox, Wiccans celebrate the second harvest. Nature is preparing for winter. Mabon is a vestige of ancient harvest festivals that, in some form or another, were once nearly universal among peoples of the Earth.

Macrocosm: The world around us.

Magick: Using knowledge and focused will to direct or re-direct energy, and manifest a change in physical reality. Any intentional act is an act of magick. It has been described as the art of wielding the power to change the course of events in one's own life. A world view which gives precedence to immanence rather than transcendence.

Magick Circle: A sphere constructed of personal power in which rituals are performed. Within it, the practitioner is protected from outside forces. The sphere extends both above and below the surface of the ground.

Magickal Correspondences: Items, objects, days, colors, moon phases, oils, angels, and herbs used in a ritual or magickal working that match the intent or purpose of the celebration or ceremony.

Malkuth: The Kingdom or Bride, the tenth sephirah; related to earth, the total manifestation of all matter.

Meditation: Reflection, contemplation - turning inward toward the self, or outward toward The Divine or nature. Quiet times in which the practitioner may either dwell upon particular thoughts or symbols, or allow them to come unbidden.

Microcosm: The world within us or humankind as a whole.

Midsummer: The Summer Solstice, usually near or on June 21, one of the eight Wiccan solar festivals. Midsummer marks the point of the year when the Sun is symbolically at the height of its powers. This is the longest day of the year. This Sabbat was Christianized by the Roman Catholic Church as St. John the Baptist Day.

Monotheism: Belief in one supreme deity who has no other forms and/or displays no other aspects.

Mother: The supernal female parent figure of the Divine, the Goddess, Lady Divine, Our Heavenly Mother, the Christian Goddess, representing motherhood, mid-life, and fertility. The full moon, the egg, and the colors red and green represent her.

Mysticism: Any method designed to bring the practitioner closer to Union with their higher self is mystical. A world view which gives precedence to transcendence rather than immanence.

Myth: Body of lore about any land or people that makes up their mythology. Neo-Pagan: Literally, a 'new Pagan'. General term for followers of traditional Wicca, Shamanism, and other polytheistic earth-based religions.

New Age: The current mixing of metaphysical practices with a structured religions, be it Christian, Jewish, Islamic, Hindu, Muslim, Buddhist.

New Moon: The Moon when it is not illuminated by direct sunlight.

Old Religion: The original name for Wicca.

Ostara: Occurring at the Spring Equinox, around March 21, Ostara marks the beginning of true, astronomical spring, when snow and ice make way for green. Ostara was Christianized by the Roman Catholic Church and is now known as Easter. It is a fertility festival, celebrating the Holy Union of the Male and Female Principles of The Divine, thus resulting in the fertility of the Earth and all creation we see around us.

Pagan: From the Latin *paganus*, "country dweller." One who practices a religion that is not part of the mainstream of Judaism, Christianity, Islam, often including Hinduism, and Buddhism.

Pantheon: A collection or group of Gods and Goddesses in a particular religious or mythical structure.

Pantheism: Belief in the faces and forms of the Divine. Paganism is pantheistic.

Paraclete: an advocate, intercessor, or pleader; in Protestant Christianity, the Holy Spirit is seen as the comforter, intercessor, and/or the advocate. In Catholicism, the Blessed Virgin Mary is the intercessor between humanity and the Holy Trinity.

Passing Over Ritual: A ritual observed by traditional Wiccans when a loved one has died.

Past Life Regression: Act of using meditation or guided meditation to pass through the veil of linear time and perceive experiences encountered in a previous existence.

Path Working: Using astral projection, bi-location, or dreamtime to accomplish a specific goal; also called vision questing.

Pendulum: A divinatory device consisting of a string attached to a heavy object, such as a quartz crystal, root, or ring. The free end of the string is held in the hand, the elbows steadied against a flat surface, and a question is asked. The movement of the heavy object's swings determines the answer. It is a tool, which contacts the psychic mind.

Pentacle/Pentagram: A circle surrounding a five-pointed, upright star (pentagram); it is often worn as a symbol of a Wiccan or The Old Religion. The basic interlaces five-pointed star, visualized with one point up. It represents the five elements: Earth, Air, Fire, Water, and Spirit. It is a symbol of power and protection. It defines the macrocosm of The Divine with the outward Circle and the Star the microcosmic Man, as depicted by Leonardo da Vinci. The circle represents: unity or the world. It also stands for the 5 wounds of Christ suffered on the cross of Calvary: the crown of thorns, the lashes to the back, nails thru the wrists, nails through the feet, and the final spear that pierced the side.

Personal Power: The energy that sustains our bodies. It originates within The Divine. We first absorb it from our biological mother within the womb, and later from food, water, the Moon and Sun, and other natural objects. You may also consider "will power" as personal power.

Planetary Hours: A system of hourly division associated with planetary energies.

Polarity: The concept of equal, opposite energies. The Eastern Yin Yang is a perfect example. Yin is cold; yang is hot. Other examples: Goddess/God, night/day, Moon/Sun, birth/death, dark/light, and psychic mind/conscious mind.

Polytheism: The belief system involving the existence of many unrelated deities each with their own dominion and interests who have no spiritual or familial relationships to one another.

Priest: A male dedicated to both the service of The Holy Trinity and humankind. All male Wiccans are priests after they have been initiated either by self-dedication rites as a solitaire or within a worship Circle. There may be a High Priest who acts as leader or and directs the rituals.

Priestess: A female dedicated to both the service of The Holy Trinity and humankind. All female Wiccans are priestesses after they have been initiated either by self-dedication rites as a solitaire or within a worship Circle. The person who acts as leader and directs the rituals.

Projective Hand: The 'dominant' hand through which personal power is sent from the body. Normally the hand used for manual activities such as writing, dialing the phone, etc.

Psychic Mind: The subconscious or unconscious mind, in which we receive psychic impressions. It is at work when we sleep, dream, and meditate. It is our direct link with the Divine, and with the larger, nonphysical world around us.

Psychism: The act of being consciously psychic, in which the psychic mind and conscious mind are linked and working in harmony. Also known as psychic awareness.

Qabala: See Kabbalah

Qliphoth: The plural of qliphah, meaning shells, or "otherness." Sometimes erroneously and patriarchally called "woman." The shadow side of sephiroth on the Trees of Life. The qliphoth are the realms of demons.

Quarters: The cardinal directions, corresponding to the Elements and protected by the Guardians. Also, know as the regents, the corners, the watchtowers, and quadrants.

Receptive Hand: The hand through which energy is drawn into the body. The left hand in right-handed persons, the reverse for left-handed persons. The receptive hand is the recessive hand.

Rede: "An' it harm none, do what thou will." The eight word philosophy of honor, ethics, and practice among all traditions of Wicca.

Reincarnation: The process of repeated incarnations in human form to allow evolution of the sexless, ageless soul. This is a post-mortem belief that souls do not end at death, but wait for a time and then are reborn to live and learn on this earth again. In the Trinitarian tradition of Wicca, this is a personal choice belief, as not all can verify past life regressions and many do not advocate this process.

Ritual: In religion, a ritual is synonymous with a ceremony and geared toward a union of the practitioner with the Divine.

Ritual Consciousness: This is a specific and alternate state of awareness is achieved using visualization and ritual. The conscious mind becomes attuned with the psychic mind, a state in which the practitioner senses energies, gives them purpose, and releases them toward a specific goal. It is a heightening of senses, an expanded awareness of the nonphysical world, a linking with nature, and communing with the Divine.

Ritual Tools: General name for tools used by a solitaire or a Circle member during their worship ceremonies or rituals. They vary by tradition and usually represent one of the elements.

Ruach: The feminine Hebrew noun meaning "Spirit."

Runes: A set of symbols used both in divination and in spiritual work.

Sabbat: One of the eight holidays that Wiccans celebrate. A holy day observed by reverence, feasting, partying, and merrymaking.

Samhain: A Wiccan festival celebrated on October 31, also known as November Eve, Hallowmas, Halloween, Feast of Souls, Feast of the Dead, Feast of Apples. Samhain marks the symbolic Death of the Sun God and His passing into the "land of the young" where he awaits re-birth at Yule. This Celtic word is pronounced by Wiccans as: SOW-wen; SEW-wen; SAHM-hain; SAHM-ain; SAV-een and other ways. The first seems to be the one preferred among most Wiccans. This festival is considered the Wiccan New Year.

Scrying: A divination method of contacting your inner self. Scrying is the act of gazing into an object (a quartz crystal sphere, a pool of water, reflections, a candle flame) while stilling the conscious mind in order to contact the psychic mind. Scrying allows the scryer to become aware of events before their actual occurrence, as well as to perceive past or present events through other than the five senses.

Sephirah: Number, immanation, sphere, or container. This is the name given to each sphere of cosmic manifestation on the Tree of Life.

Sephiroth: The plural of sephirah.

Shaman: A man or woman who has obtained knowledge of the subtler dimensions of the Earth, usually through periods of alternate states of consciousness. Various types of ritual allow the shaman to pierce the veil of the physical world and to experience the realm of energies. This knowledge lends the shaman the power to change his or her world through higher perception.

Shamanism: The spiritual practices of shamans, or the Native American form of communing with The Divine, usually ritualistic and religious in nature.

Shekinah: The female embodiment of spiritual power.

Shrine: A sacred place that holds a collection of objects representing a deity; akin to a temple, a monument, or sacred ground.

Sigil: A seal, sign, glyph, or other marking used to denote a specific group, tradition, Circle, or individual. Self-created sigils are the most effective and can be used on letters, packages, clothing, etc.

Solitary: A Wiccan of any tradition who studies, works, and worships alone.

Solstice: The time of the sun's passing a solstice, which occurs about June 22 to begin summer and about December 22 to begin winter in the Northern Hemisphere.

Sophia: The Goddess of Wisdom, acknowledged by the Greeks and the Gnostic Christians.

Spell: Spells can best be explained as prayers with props. They should be clear, concise, focused, and emotional. It is the extension of mental and emotional energy in order to accomplish a specific goal.

Spiral: This symbol signifies an inward journey. It represents the emergence into consciousness of what was previously hidden. It also suggests the round of seasons, where life unfolds and fades, unfolds again in a repeating cycle - it means life.

Spirit: The overall one limitless, genderless energy that runs the universe in a harmonious way. As with any term, it has many names: the fifth element, The All, Akasha, and YHWH.

Staff: Ritual tool which corresponds to the wand or athame.

Subconscious Mind: Part of the mind which functions below the levels we are able to access in the course of a normal working day. This area stores symbolic knowledge, dreams, the minutest details of every experience ever had by a person.

Summerland: The Pagan or Wiccan equivalent to Heaven.

Supernal Triad: The third sephiroth above the abyss, which is the source of all creation.

Sympathetic Magick: Concept of like attracts like. Most common way spells are worked.

Talisman: An object charged with personal spiritual power to attract a specific force or energy to its bearer; often worn as amulets and shields of protection.

Tetragrammaton: YHVH or IHVH. The four-letter name of the Deity commonly referred to as Yahweh. Tetragrammaton contains a complex formula relating to cosmic union and the manifestation of the elements. Only after the creation is manifest is the term YHVH is used for God in the Bible.

Threefold Law: Karmic principle that energy that is sent forth on this realm is returned to the practitioner three; this applies to good and bad energy as well as both usages of prayers and spells.

Tiphareth: Beauty, the sixth and central sephirah on the middle pillar of the Tree of Life, related to both male and female, and the central core or heart of each individual.

Traditions: An organized, structured, specific Wiccan sub-group. This term is synonymous with Christian Church denominations.

Trance: An altered state of consciousness; the basis for meditation, visualization and many forms of out of the body experiences.

Transcendence: The belief or experience that The Divine is separate, not manifested in each human. It is found through acts that separate us from mundane reality.

Tree of Life: this is the 10 sephiroth and the 22 connecting paths. All forms - manifest, common, uncommon, animated, and unanimated - mirror structure.

Triple Goddess: The earliest belief systems of the Trinity were all feminine; One Goddess in all of her three aspects: Maiden, Mother, and Crone. This aspect of three important females is also represented in Christianity with the Trinity of Marys. Christianity the first patriarchal Trinity, however through research that aspect has changed to include a God the Father, God the Mother, and God the Holy Son.

Vision Quest: In modern times, this refers to the process of using astral projection, bi-location, or dreamtime to accomplish a specific goal or to visit another person. Also called path working, Its origins are noted in the shamanistic ways of the Native American Indians.

Visualization: The process of forming mental images. Visualization consists of forming images of needed goals during ritual. It is also used to direct personal power and natural energies for various purposes.

Wand: A ritual tool representing the element of fire.

Waning Moon: A phase of the moon in which the face of the moon appears to be getting smaller (the time between a full moon and a new moon).

Warlock: An antiquated term misused in reference to a male witch; as it means 'oath-breaker', 'liar', or 'betrayer'. Most male Wiccans find the use of this term very offensive.

Water: In most Wiccan traditions, this element corresponds with the direction of west, the color blue, the psychic properties of the mind, intuition, and emotion. When working with angels or in Angel Wicca, Gabriel governs the west and its representation.

Waxing Moon: The phase of the moon in which the face of the moon appears to be getting larger (the time between a new moon and a full moon).

Wheel of the Year: The full cycle of the eight Sabbats in the Wiccan calendar. They occur at the Equinoxes and Solstices (the Quarters) and on the days marking the midpoints between them (the Cross-Quarters.)

Wicca: an earth-reaffirming religion with ritual observance of the lunar timetable, agricultural times for planting and harvesting, and the changes of the seasons.

Wiccan Rede: The shortened 8-word moral, magickal, and ethical code of all who practice Wicca: "An' it harm none, do what ye will."

Wicce: Synonymous with Wicca. In some circles, Wicce is used for women and Wicca is used for men.

Widdershins: Counterclockwise motion. When casting a worship circle clockwise, it is erroneous to consider it for negative magickal purposes, or for dispersing negative energies or conditions such as disease. Deosil is consider for positive actions. This applies only in the Northern Hemisphere. In the Southern Hemisphere, these actions and purposes are reversed. However, in reality, both directions are only symbolic and neither automatically invokes good or bad energy. Trinitarian Wiccans may wish to cast Esbats by Widdershins for positive reaffirmation of the female aspect of the Christian Holy Trinity.

Witch: A practitioner of the Craft. This term applies equally to either males or females. Originally, a European practitioner of pre-Christian folk magick, particularly that kind relating to herbs, stones, colors, wells, rivers, etc. This term has been deliberately altered to denote dangerous supernatural beings who practiced destructive magick and who threatened Christianity.

Witchcraft: The craft of the witch - magick, especially magick utilizing personal power in conjunction with the energies within stones, herbs, colors, and other natural objects. An alternative term for Wicca, the Old Religion, and the religion of the wise.

Yesod: Foundation, the tenth sephirah, related to the feminine; astral and sexual energy. Also the place where the unresolved subconscious material is deposited in the individual and collective psyche.

Yetzirah: The third world of formation, the realm of angels.

Yule: A Wiccan festival celebrated on or about December 21, marking the re-birth of the Sun God from the Earth Goddess. It is a time of joy and celebration during the miseries of winter. Yule occurs on the Winter Solstice.

About the Author:

Nancy Chandler-Pittman is a 40-year-old ChristoPagan author who celebrates her zeal for Wicca and magick through the Kabbalistic-Gnostic Pantheons. She is an ordained Interfaith Minister, with an Honorary Doctorate in Divinity from the Universal Life Church. Born on July 4, Nancy's personality has formed as an independent thinker. She is also a musician, an author, a teacher, and is in some senses a spiritual rebel. She has always followed her own heart toward methods of communing with the Genderless Spirit.

A songwriter/musician since her early teens, she has written and produced several albums, and has founded an independent record label and distribution company. From 1983 until 1998, Nancy traveled extensively, performing and promoting her music. She has been featured regularly in major magazines and independent publications.

Passionate about the Tarot and mysticism since age 14, Nancy teaches a 36-week class on the Rider-Waite Tarot deck, stressing the Tree of Life, Jungian philosophies, numerology, and the Hebrew alphabet. Now owning her own occult store, the Shadows and Light Shoppe, she encourages spiritual tolerance in the magickal community in North Alabama.

Nancy also teaches Wicca through open circles using a hands-on approach to coven work. She teaches the celebrations of the Sabbats and Esbats from various Pagan traditions, combined with non-dogmatic Christianity. Nancy firmly believes that magico-religious tolerance will be achieved through the studies of parallel philosophies, and comparative spiritual research. Nancy holds true to these ethics in her teachings and life.